# our help in ages past

our help in ages past

# the black church's ministry among the elderly

bobby joe saucer
with jean alicia elster

JUDSON PRESS
PUBLISHERS SINCE 1824

VALLEY FORGE, PENNSYLVANIA

OUR HELP IN AGES PAST
The Black Church's Ministry among the Elderly
© 2005 by Judson Press, Valley Forge, PA 19482-0851
All rights reserved.

Judson Press has made every effort to trace the ownership of all quotes. In the event of a question arising from the use of a quote, we regret any error made and will be pleased to make the necessary correction in future printings and editions of this book.

The Scripture quotations contained herein are from the from the New American Standard Bible, © 1960, 1962, 1963, 1968, 1971, 1972, 1973, 1975, 1977 by The Lockman Foundation. Used by permission.

Library of Congress Cataloging-in-Publication Data

Saucer, Bobby Joe.
Our help in ages past : the Black church's ministry among the elderly / Bobby Joe Saucer ; with Jean Alicia Elster, ed. p. cm.
Includes bibliographical references.
ISBN 0-8170-1483-7 (alk. paper)
1. Church work with older people. 2. African American churches. I. Elster, Jean Alicia. II. Title.
BV4435.S28 2005
259'.3'08996073—dc22
                                                    2005002482

Printed in the U.S.A.

12 11 10 09 08 07 06
10 9 8 7 6 5 4 3 2

Dedicated to
the riveting memory
of my mother,
Mrs. Marguerite
Delores Jackson Paster

CONTENTS

# ACKNOWLEDGEMENTS

The reflections presented in these pages are a compilation of infusions from the lives and kind mercies of others. I did not and could not earn the privileges that have served as the foundation of my life. I will never be able to recall nor remember to thank them all. But yet "new mercies" from their "sacred and precious memories" continue to energize my grateful heart. As a testimony of my gratitude, "May the work [I do] speak for me."

Those to whom I owe a debt of gratitude include my wife, Elois Wyche Saucer; my children, Marcus Keith Cobb Saucer, Alnita LeJoyce Wyche Saucer, and Jason Jerome Jackson Saucer; my four brothers, Leo Samuel, Anderson Samuel III, Millard Dean, and William Caleb; and my mentors and friends Dr. Gardner C. Taylor, Dr. James Hal Cone, Dr. Eddie S. O'Neal, and Dr. David A. Anderson.

I am also grateful for the influences of my late grandfather Rev. Anderson Samuel Jackson Sr., and my grandmother, the late Mrs. Irene May Jackson; of my wife's late grandparents Mr. Sam Washington and Mrs. Viola Wooten Washington, and of my late father-in-law, Mr. Zelma C. Wyche. I thank God for my mother-in-law, Mrs. Myrtle W. Wyche, from whose pilgrimage we continue to harvest great and unique "pearls of wisdom."

I owe an eternal debt of gratitude to my friend and brother, Dr. Jesse F. McClure. His critiques and counsel have enriched my reflections for more than thirty-three years.

I also remain indebted to my undergraduate department chair and surrogate father, the late Dr. Henry Earl Cobb, who continues to influence my point of view and vision of new worlds and possibilities, and to his widow, Dr. Thelma M. Cobb.

To these and many others who are worthy of being mentioned and acknowledged, thank you.

—Bobby Joe Saucer

*Do not cast me off in the time of old age; do not forsake
me when my strength is spent.* —Psalm 71:9

While reflecting on the plight of the African American elderly, one
can safely conclude that there is no single model that represents the
communities in which they reside and the churches in which they
worship—all have their unique differences and distinctions. In fact,
the ever-growing presence of the black elderly provides challenges
and opportunities for the growth, development, and empowerment of African American communities *wherever* the elderly reside
and worship.

Given the resourcefulness and resiliency of ministries that are
reflected in the historical records of African American churches, it
is clear that these churches have striven to witness and lead. They
can—and will—continue to advocate and champion causes that
address the needs of their constituencies. Their histories give ample
reason for such hope and optimism. More specifically, the history
of advocacy within these churches is a rich and noble one. It ought
to be expanded! In that respect, a focus on the aging and elderly
can potentially launch a movement that has implications for the
advancement of African American communities in particular and
American society as a whole in situations where needs are evident
and, sometimes, epidemic.

Therefore, the purpose of *Our Help in Ages Past: The Black
Church's Ministry among the Elderly* is to sound the call for a
greater awareness of both the needs and the opportunities associated with ministry to the elderly in the church. This book challenges the church to acknowledge and act upon its responsibility to
address the many and varied needs of those who have gone before,
people whose sacrifices and commitments have made the church
what it is today. This book suggests and urges a process—within
the African American church—for creative relationships between
the elderly and those who are younger. It is hoped that such

relationships will encourage dialogue, mentoring, nurturing, affirmation, encouragement, and empowerment.

Embracing the maxim "knowledge is power," elderly blacks represent the power sources of wisdom in African American churches. All other age groups benefit as a result of heightened sensitivity toward the needs of the elderly. Therefore, this book also invites the church to explore and savor the wisdom older people have to offer, wisdom that might be lost if not properly recognized, recorded, and incorporated into the lifeblood of the church and its members.

Unfortunately, a significant percentage of African Americans have been estranged from the religious and service-oriented experiences of the church. With the creation of ministries to the elderly that blend the traditions and practices of the church with *new* ministries that engage the energies, gifts, and skills of the younger generations, these disconnected generations can be reintroduced and reconnected in a meaningful way within the church. Such a process can lead to partnerships based on relationships that are self-perpetuating and reinvigorating to young and old alike.

Finally, this book is an invitation to recognize and employ the many ministry gifts that older people have to offer. Sometimes, meaningful senior ministry to others entails first finding opportunities for the elderly to contribute their spiritual gifts and secular talents to the church and its mission. Finding such opportunities requires a focus and resolve by pastors, lay leaders, and congregations to pursue the vision of allowing the elderly to serve the church and for the church to advocate and support the elderly.

Sensitivity, intentionality, and advocacy become building blocks in creating ministries that serve the elderly within the church. As with all things worthwhile, the process will require careful attention, thought, planning, and training. However, in the interest of the vitality and integrity of church life and mission, the contents of this book are offered to both pastors and laypersons as a blueprint for creating vital and engaging ministries to the elderly within our churches.

# CHAPTER 1

# Who Are the African American Elderly?

I have been young, and now am old.
—Psalm 37:25*a*

As the African American church prepares to address new challenges in the twenty-first century, it is incumbent upon the church's current and future leaders to engage in a new, more comprehensive view of its future mission and ministries. African American church leaders must guide the church in developing a plan of service that maintains its past history of ministry while acknowledging the existence of an aging population that presents new and radically different challenges and needs.

The responsibilities of the "sandwich" generation—those who fulfill the duties of caring for both the young and the elderly—will increasingly tax the physical strength of caregivers, the economic resources of wage earners, and the home environment in which the individuals live. The adequacy of the family to sustain its pivotal role of care is an issue of grave importance. Without the ministry of support provided by the African American church, the task will be daunting, if not impossible.

The future of many aging blacks is clouded by their history of employment in sectors of the labor force that did not provide retirement benefits. It is only natural that advocacy for the welfare and well-being of this segment of older black Americans becomes the primary responsibility of the African American church. The role of the black church as advocate and defender of older black Americans must become the foundation of its ministry and Christian education emphasis. The church must sensitize and educate its congregations into a new and more deliberate consciousness. The lives and pilgrimages of our senior members contain vital content for the survival, renewal, and progress of younger African Americans. Void of their genius to persevere and thrive, the race would have already perished.

## Consider This

United States Census Bureau statistics indicate that for the year 2001, nearly three million African Americans were sixty-five years of age or older. This group represents 8.5 percent of *all* Americans sixty-five or older during that year. Thirty-nine and one-half percent of elderly blacks are male and 60.5 percent are female. From 2001 to 2021, the elderly black population is projected to grow by 89.6 percent. When extrapolated out to 2041, population growth of older African Americans is projected to increase by 220.4 percent! In fact, according to the Census Bureau's 2002 Population Projections Program, the African American aged population is expected to increase nearly three times that of the white elderly population between the years 2001 and 2041. The survival rate of older African American men is projected to improve from the current 39.5 percent to 42.4 percent by the year 2041.

In order to become a formidable advocate, the African American church must be armed with a critical mass of data and projections. Without this data to analyze, the church will not be equipped to play an essential role of advocacy and planning. This data will greatly help leaders—pastors, deacons, trustees, church school teachers, and Vacation Bible School leaders—understand the numerical realities that will support their ministries for black seniors. A truly effective witness will require both information and inspiration.

As the percentage of the black elderly increases faster than all other age groups in our communities, what will happen to the status of their

■ health

■ income

■ employment opportunities

■ living arrangements

■ housing

■ transportation

■ life options

■ overall quality of life?

These concerns challenge the African American church to perform its unique role of public policy review. The church must propose and monitor programs that have an impact on the aging population.

## "Prosper and Be in Health..."

The economic plight of black seniors is a major factor in determining their quality of life. Currently, Social Security benefits are the primary source of income for older blacks. In 1999 Social Security accounted for nearly one half (47.1 percent) of the total income for the black elderly. Retirement income from pensions ranked second (20 percent), and earned income represented 17.7 percent. Social Security income constituted seven times as much of the aggregate income of elderly blacks as their white counterparts. In 1999 half of all African American seniors had income levels below $10,000.

Even more telling, the poverty profile is compounded for older blacks who are within the Census Bureau category of "unrelated living alone." African American seniors living without relatives and in isolation are worse off financially. They also represent the most economically deprived groups in the entire society. That same census data tells us that in 1999, 43.8 percent of unrelated black females sixty-five years of age or older living alone were poor. Factoring in the income categories of the poor, the marginally poor, or the economically vulnerable, nearly four out of every five older, unrelated black females living alone were poor. For aged blacks, seven out of every ten were poor.

It is crucial that the African American church grasp the far-reaching social impact of the income status of black seniors in order to determine how to respond most effectively to their needs. The income statistics mentioned above have significant economic implications for our own local communities as well as for the society at large.

Closely related to income status is the issue of living arrangements. According to data in "America's Families and Living Arrangements: March 2000," in 1998 only about 36 percent of all African Americans aged sixty-five or older lived with a spouse. Approximately 35 percent of all older African Americans lived alone; 25 percent lived with a relative other than a spouse, and 4 percent lived with nonrelatives. In fact, older blacks are twice as likely to live with a relative other than a spouse than they are to live with a spouse!

Regarding African American seniors and the status of their health, an October 1999 report published by the Centers for Disease Control and Prevention states that four out of every ten elderly blacks reported their health status as poor or just fair. Roughly three out of ten reported that their health was good or excellent. From 1996 data, elderly blacks reported 97 percent more sick days of bed confinement than elderly whites did.

Life expectancy at birth in 1998 for African American males was 67.6 years. For African American females, life expectancy was 74.8 years. However, if older blacks do survive to age sixty-five, then their life expectancy increases; black women can expect

4

to live to the age of 82.4 years, and black men can expect to live to the age of 79.3 years. While this latter data is encouraging, older African American men still die at an earlier age than African American women.

For the black elderly, there have been few, if any, social, fraternal, or other organizational sources or structures of support. Thus the role and potential role of the African American church with respect to black seniors is not only pivotal but urgent. Not until the church becomes the astute responder to the needs of those with callused hands, receding hairlines, graying sideburns, fallen arches, stooped backs, and dimming eyesight will the future offer sustained hope for our elder members. It behooves the church to remember that, as those who have been willing to "fight the good fight and finish the race" (see 2 Timothy 4:7), our senior brothers and sisters deserve all of the creativity, compassion, and support we can muster on their behalf.

## Where Do You Stand?

Review the information in Appendix One, then bring that information home with the following:

1. List some "senior citizens" with whom you share close relationships.

2. Looking at that list, describe, as best you can, the lifestyles of those seniors.

3. To all appearances, what is their health status?

4. Assess your current health status.

5. What do you foresee as your health status as an older person?

6. How do you envision your lifestyle when you are sixty-five or older?

## Models for Action

Who are the African American elderly as *you* see them? Complete the following lists. Some suggestions have been given; change or add to them as you see fit.

The elderly fulfill roles as—
■ Parents
■ Grandparents
■
■
■
■

Within the church, seniors fulfill the duties of—
■ Ushers
■ Sunday school teachers
■
■
■
■

Within society in general, the elderly participate as—
■ Volunteers
■ Mentors
■
■
■

The status of seniors within society might be as—
■ Retirees
■ Consultants
■
■
■
■

Their places of residence can be—
■ Single-family homes
■ Apartments
■
■
■
■

Their previous professions were as—
■ Laborers
■ Teachers
■
■
■
■

Their current professions might be as—
■ Cooks
■ Clerks
■
■
■
■

CHAPTER 2

# The African American Church's Responsibility to the Elderly

*There was not a needy person among them...*
—Acts 4:34*a*

Even though we are now in the twenty-first century, most of the seniors who are members of our African American churches still remember an America of Jim Crow and a culture that accepted as normal the cruel indignities that accompanied segregation and racial discrimination. The phrase *politically correct* did not exist for most of their lives. And it was not so long ago that the black church offered one of the few sanctuaries from the harsh restrictions of racism in American society.

It was in the black church that adult men were addressed as "Mr." and adult women were addressed as "Mrs." Men, who were for the most part systematically barred from professions where a suit was the required attire, could wear a tailored suit on Sunday morning. Women, who might have donned a head scarf in doing "day work," walked up to the sanctuary with beautifully coiffed hair. Those who may not have had the opportunity to get a good or "equal" education and attend colleges and universities rose up the ranks to positions of leadership within the church as elders, deacons, deaconesses, ushers, Sunday school teachers, and trustees. They may not have had access to jobs that allowed them to contribute to retirement plans, but they made sacrifices for the sake of their church family and made contributions to the life and future of the church. At one urban church, founding members were able to pay off the church mortgage by periodically pledging a full week's pay to the church building fund!

And even for those who *were* able to break through some of the constraints of racism and attain a certain level of the "American dream," the black church offered a place to hone their talents, perfect their skills, and earn their stripes. One gentleman who became a well-respected public school administrator and a dynamic public speaker perfected his oratory skills while reciting the poems of Paul Laurence Dunbar at church pageants. Others who were able to attend Howard University School of Law or Meharry Medical School welcomed church members as their first clients or patients.

To those for whom the church formed such an integral and life-affirming part of their existence and for whom the church offered respite from the harsh realities of racial injustice, we owe them no less than to continue addressing their needs and advocating on their behalf during their elder years.

## Consider This

Older African Americans—by virtue of their survival and dogged determination to persevere and overcome—represent the "survival of the fittest." A lifetime of making do and doing without has brought them to us as a treasured gift to be mined for their courage, determination, ingenuity, and hope for the difficult days yet to be faced by people of color in the United States. In the Spring 2001 issue of *The African American Pulpit*, I cited AARP's 1995 "Minority Affairs" in stating, "The status and resources of many minorities reflect social and economic discrimination experienced in earlier life. As a consequence, the black elderly are at increased risk for poor education, substandard housing, malnutrition, and generally poor health status." (p. 21–22) All of the socioeconomic practices visited upon older blacks in the marketplace of earlier periods of their lives continue to affect their existence in their seasons of waning energy and dwindling strength. These included policies and practices of:

■ underemployment
■ work in the most backbreaking and health-challenging sectors of the workforce
■ the last hired and the first fired
■ unequal pay for equal or greater production
■ poor-quality and hazardous workplaces
■ lack of healthcare and disability benefits
■ lack of pension or retirement benefits

All these served to contribute to the plight and pilgrimage of older African Americans.

## "Who Will Go for Us?"

Black seniors need someone to represent them in the halls of public policy and program formulation. They need someone to represent them in arenas where goods and services are distributed. Given the cultural pattern of voluntary organizational participation and membership, the African American church is the logical *advocate*.

Other racial and ethnic groups have enjoyed the supportive services of voluntary agencies and organizations all along their life continuum. For the most part, those older African Americans who have had the quality of their lives impacted by nonfamilial support have had it come via their relationship with and involvement in the black church.

Literature and research, in the main, would seem to argue against such a role for the church because of findings that portend a less than revered and respectable status and role for older people in the church. A cursory review of the writings on the status and role of the elderly in the church leaves one with the distinct impression that older members are marginalized and even ostracized and that, therefore, they are no longer a valued and vital part of the focused mission and ministries of the church. This marginalization is suggested by the different losses visited on human beings as part of the aging process. Thus, seniors are marginalized as members because of lack of hearing acumen; marginalized because of the dwindling presence of their peers; and marginalized in terms of the program and budget allocations for ministries for, to, and with aging and aged groupings in the church.

These studies, for the most part, reflect observations and findings of the status and role of older members in nonblack church settings. These descriptors, therefore, may not reflect African American church settings. While black churches can, in some cases, reflect this age-exclusion behavior, overall the practice of exclusion would be an aberration—a radical departure from the cultural norm. Generally within African American churches, senior members are neither expected nor forced to relinquish positions of leadership just because of age. In fact, in most cases seniors are venerated.

If we consider the long tenures of pastoral leadership and the advanced age of those leaders as we see them active in the life of the congregation, it is safe to conclude that ageism is not as prevalent in the leadership configuration and structure of most black churches as it may be in other cultural settings. The length of pastoral leadership and the advanced age of that tenured pastor, coupled with the lengthy history of a congregation's existence, tend to be reflected in the leadership of the laity and the ages of elected and appointed office holders. In fact, an older person's influence in both the church and the black community is usually in direct proportion to the tenure of pastoral leadership. In other words, the older the pastor—and the longer the tenure in a particular pulpit—the more likely you are to find other elder members of the church in key positions of leadership.

The central and pivotal role of the black church in the life of the African American community in general, and in the lives of older blacks in particular, argues persuasively for the role of advocacy in the black church. While some churches are sensitive to the presence and plight of the black elderly, they must become more intentional both in their sensitivity and in their focused commitment. This intentionality has to be reflected by a pervasive, programmatic sensitivity to the need for resource allocation and deployment of those resources in ministries of advocacy. In order to achieve this intentionality, both personal and corporate commitments are essential.

## "Commit Your Cause to the Lord"

A personal commitment requires a resolve to become a scholar of fallen arches, careful observer of slowed gaits, a student of callused hands, a historian of furrowed countenances, a podiatrist of tired feet, an ophthalmologist of diminishing visual focus, a dentist of creative denture needs, and an interpreter of receding hairlines. Crucial opportunities for ministry with the elderly can revolve around very simple matters of daily life. As such, these opportunities can also be easily missed.

The corporate commitment—that of the black church—must take the form of advocacy: advocating for senior-sensitive public policies, for creative and viable services and service-delivery systems, and for rights and privileges that address the need for an improved quality of life.

Several areas urgently beckon for the church's concern, sensitivity, commitment, and response. One such urgent area is the need for sensitivity to and relief for caregivers of elderly relatives who are maintained in or relocated to the home of that caregiver. Added to such a ministry of outreach must be assistance in the areas of
■ nutrition
■ adequate, safe, and accessible housing

■ transportation

■ affordable healthcare

In the arena of volunteerism, there has existed historically a natural relationship between the African American church and older blacks. This affinity has been one of necessity and survival as well as one of mutual support and benefit. While this volunteerism will serve as a valuable foundation, there will be a growing need for more intentional development of comprehensive programs that will provide services that support and improve the quality of life of senior members.

What is being suggested here is a focused ministry to, for, and with older African Americans. This requires a recognition by the total congregation of the explosive growth and presence of the elderly in families, church, community, and society as a whole.

For example, the African American church must develop and expand its ministries to those people (usually relatives) who are aiding older members of the congregation as helpers and caregivers. The initial step is a heightened sense of awareness and sensitivity, and a consistent expression of encouragement and appreciation for the caregiver. In such a ministry, the cost is low budget, but it requires committed human capital—including short- and long-term accountability, quality training by knowledgeable professionals, and a careful selection process (remembering that all congregations are blessed with an abundance of persons who are more *willing* than *able*). This must be a ministry of pastoral sensitivity, adorned with listening skills of compassion and companionship. It requires willing hands, humble hearts, and a mind to serve. In addition, those who represent this ministry must be trained and equipped to serve without risking violation of confidentiality and trust.

Congregations of every size, location, and varying resources can plan, design, and implement a ministry of relief that eases the burden placed upon the caregiver. In such a ministry of relief, however, the church should be mindful of the time and tenure requested of its volunteers. Will the commitment be for a morning, an afternoon, or an evening? Will it be a weekly, monthly, or just occasional commitment? Highly specialized and skilled members of a compassionate congregation may be available only for a few hours per week or even per month. That is fine. The church can be instrumental in initiating, facilitating, and coordinating a schedule for volunteers and the caregivers in a congregation. Even one or two hours of planned relief time for each caregiver will prove golden. The value in such a ministry is derived from planned and anticipated time intervals of relief for caregivers who, otherwise, are cut off from the congregation and the community and who, while laboring in love, grow weary in silence. A proactive ministry of relief can also remove the psychological feeling of guilt when a caregiver admits to weariness and fatigue.

Another vital area of service to the elderly is assistance in simple daily activities. Tasks such as retrieving mail can prove daunting in residential areas that present barriers such as distance, stairs, inclines, post office boxes, and the like. Assistance in reading, interpreting, and understanding mail from the government, banks, and medical providers can be both liberating and empowering. Assistance with the payment of property taxes and calculating the homestead tax exemption constitutes a major blessing in the quality of life for our aging members.

The statistical profile of the African American elderly provides clarity about both the challenges and opportunities that beckon for the mission and ministries of the black church. No matter the size, location, or resource limitations, all religious assemblages have one pivotal resource in abundance—human capital. Recently, this author attended the congresses of Christian education of the National Baptist Convention of America, Inc., the National Baptist Convention USA, Inc., and the Progressive National Baptist Convention, Inc. These meetings were attended primarily by youth, young adults, church school teachers, and ministers. They numbered in excess of 12,000 and 40,000 people respectively. What a source of human capital that needs to be focused and refocused! They have to be trained and taught to raise the poignant inquiries:

■ Who and where are the black elderly?
■ How are they faring?
■ What are their needs?
■ How might I become involved in a ministry of knowledge, sensitivity, commitment, and advocacy?

In Chapter 8, several activities observed over the years by this author will be shared as models of the ministry of sensitivity, outreach, and service.

# Where Do You Stand?

Take some time to review the vignettes in Appendix Two and then consider the following:

1. How would you expect the church to respond to your needs when you are older?

2. What are some realistic expectations of how the African American church should respond to the needs of seniors?

3. How would you describe the African American church's greatest strengths in outreach to its older members?

4. What are the African American church's greatness weaknesses in outreach to the elderly?

## Models for Action

It's your turn! List the African American seniors that you know who have been strengthened by the ministries of the church.

- 
- 
- 
- 

What were some of those ministries?

- 
- 
- 
- 

List the older African American who have had *their* gifts developed through activities within the church.

- 
- 
- 
- 

List the African American seniors who have selflessly contributed to their church.

- 
- 
- 
- 

What are some examples of their contributions?

- 
- 
- 
-

What older African American has most affected your life and why?

# CHAPTER 3

# God's Call to Care

Honor your father and your mother, so that your days may
be long in the land that the LORD your God is giving you.
—Exodus 20:12

In God's Word, there is a clear connection between obedience to
God and respect for the oldest members of our communities.
Certainly, there is no legitimate justification for our churches to
ignore the needs and gifts of our seniors. It is an honor to be called
into the presence of God and to be given a task that is both attainable and enriching. Therefore, our response to the elder members
of our community is not only important socially but also theologically. It is a direct response (or failure to respond) to the God who
establishes and upholds our faith community. Can we deny that the
lives of our oldest "saints" are important to the Creator? Does not
even a cursory study of the Scriptures reveal God's care for those
who served by paving the way before us? And should not that
divine care be manifest in our attitudes and our steps?

The study of Scripture in small groups as well as in the Sunday sermon may be necessary to establish this congregational focus of service to the elderly and to welcome the fullness of their gifts. Sometimes
people are resistant to new directions, but God's Word is clear. It may
take time, but our "fathers and mothers" are waiting.

Time is both the witness and revelation offered to us by our seniors. Spending *our time* with those who have lived through former and often difficult times can open new vistas and possibilities. Viewing life through the eyes of those who have passed this way before can reveal patterns and opportunities in situations and events that once appeared to be the result of confusion and mistakes. God has placed God's own wisdom as near to us as a home visit or a nursing home service. God's ministry touches the soul as it presses the flesh. Although getting started in such senior ministry may be hard, anyone who dedicates him or herself to activities that both nourish and are nourished by the elderly will be blessed.

Meeting people at their place of need confirms God's love. At this moment those who are precious in God's sight—the black elderly—are waiting. They are waiting to see what God will do next. Our presence in the lives of seniors will reveal God to them and will also reveal God to us. When this faithful interaction occurs, God acts, and all involved can expect a renewal of faith and the opportunity to sojourn in the presence of God through fellowship.

## Consider This

In our modern age, failing to embrace the issues of aging and of the aged would marginalize an entire cross section of the black community, which is already all too familiar with marginalization. Marginalization is a poor reward for lives that have been lived so fully for so long. The issues relating to old age are not new. Even the psalmist provides a forum for petitioning God in this matter: "Do not cast me off in the time of old age; do not forsake me when my strength is spent" (Psalm 71:9).

No one wants to be forgotten or minimized. Actions taken by the modern church can address the issues of black seniors if we place ourselves in the midst of their issues and find ourselves as participants in God's response. By creating an event or making a visit that allows an older person to feel as valuable to the congregation, community, or *us* as that individual is to the Creator, we personally act on behalf of God. In this way, we become God's presence in the lives of others and break the chains of despair that can imprison those who feel alone and unwanted. This is the worthiest of goals.

Psalm 71:13 declares, "...let those who seek to hurt me be covered in scorn and disgrace." A penalty will be paid for allowing the resource of our older people to be lost. As individuals, we must acknowledge that it is in our power to bring actual harm to our churches by ignoring the plight of those who have come before us and by overlooking what they have to offer. Theirs was a mighty task. These travelers have been down many, diverse roads over a multitude of years. Their journeys combine at this point to offer us a great spiritual opportunity. There is no room for rationalization or excuses. Those we don't help, we harm. To miss this opportunity is to harm ourselves as well. Today is a day for action. Today is a day for receiving what our elders have to give—lest we suffer the lack of that great resource.

## "I Will Hope Continually"

The busy pace of modern life can leave us feeling hopeless. Hope is around us. Hope is in our hands. Hope is in the hands of those who await us. Where do we find our hope?

The psalmist reveals that this is not a new quandary: "For you, O LORD, are my hope, my trust, O LORD, from my youth" (Psalm 71:5). Rather than expend energy trying to reinvent ourselves against the issues we think are peculiar to our days, we might better seek insight from those who know. The black elderly are veterans of coping. They have endured the trials of life and are now available as resources. Taking an hour just to be with one of our seniors will expose our restless souls to hope. The line between the one giving and the one receiving will be blurred. The blessing of presence will issue forth in the promise of hope. One sure way to receive the blessing you desire is to be a blessing to another. Hope knows no age limits.

Have you ever wondered about the amount of power you have in this world? Does it often seem like you need more? Personal power increases as it is shared. By offering ourselves, our time, and our resources to those who are at risk of neglect and powerlessness, we can help reinstitute pleasure, respect, and dignity. That's power! Seniors, like everyone else, are subject to disappointment and loneliness. The Christian call is not only to pray and hope, but to stand in the reflection of Jesus' desire for all people. In this way, we can fulfill the prayer of the psalmist who said, "You will increase my honor, and comfort me once again" (Psalm 71:21).

Personal visits—regular visitation that evolves into solid relationships—and welcoming events that celebrate strengths and express gratitude for what has been done in years gone by will all increase honor and comfort for our seniors. These actions will release God's goodness and hope into life in ways that will enhance individuals and the whole community of faith.

Echoed in the words of Exodus 20:12 and in the voice of the psalmist are messages that pervade the Scriptures. *God cares*— God cares for those at risk of marginalization. *God celebrates*— God celebrates the life of both young and old. *God does not forget*—God remembers the efforts of those who laid the foundation for our faith communities. Celebration is energized by remembrance and recognition, and demonstrated in caring and service. We, the people of God, must not fail to care. We must not cease to celebrate. We must not forget.

## Where Do You Stand?

1. In what ways can you learn of God as you reach out to the elder members of your community and allow them to reach back to you?

2. Give some examples of ways in which you have been blessed when you have worked to include someone who might otherwise have been marginalized.

3. What might you learn about yourself as you interact with the seniors in your community?

4. Do you think your church is doing an adequate job of serving God by serving those for whom God cares? Why or why not?

5. How do you imagine God will enrich your life and your church's life through service to and with the elderly?

## Models for Action

Give some examples of how God might meet you in the sacred space of visiting with an elderly friend.

■

■

■

■

Identify some specific concerns God has placed on your heart for the seniors in your community.

■

■

■

■

Identify ways you might address those concerns.

■

■

■

■

Outline some ways you can encourage your congregation to view meeting the needs of the elderly and welcoming their gifts as obedience to God.

■ Bible study

■ Sunday morning sermon

■

■

■

■

# CHAPTER 4

# Incorporating Seniors into the Life of the Church

*"...the elder shall serve the younger."*
—Genesis 25:23

For some, the title of this chapter, "Incorporating Seniors into the Life of the Church," represents a task that has already been accomplished. "From what I can see," such readers may exclaim, "the church is *full* of older people!" And while the elderly may, in many congregations, outnumber members of younger generations, are these seniors just warming pews or are they vibrant members of the life of the church?

Many older people feel they have, quite frankly, outlived their usefulness! Such persons may have no needs other than the need to be needed. Seniors who have been accustomed to being active, now—because of illness or frailty—no longer do what they used to do. How might they contribute to a ministry? Other seniors, used to performing a certain task for the church in a certain way, now find that new technologies make their contributions obsolete or at best antiquated. Longtime church school teachers may have trouble adjusting to new curricula and current teaching methods. Other churches, experiencing rapid growth, find that they want to change worship or ministry practices that may have been practiced one way for years but are now no longer effective in a remodeled church vision. Seniors, caught in the crosswinds of these changes, no longer recognize their beloved congregations.

Perhaps without realizing it, the church has ministered to its older members in ways that may not have even been viewed as being part of a ministry. For example, one retired senior volunteered in a church office twice a week. Her job was folding bulletins. She also mailed copies of the previous week's bulletin to members who were hospitalized or bedridden. She remarked, "I worked as a cook in a school cafeteria for thirty years. I was tired. I couldn't wait to retire! Then I realized how much that job meant to me....Helping out in the church office two days a week makes me feel needed. It gives me a reason to get up in the morning." Another elderly church school teacher casually remarked to a parent, "You know, I never had children of my own. But by teaching these young people over those many years, I've shared a bit in the raising of *hundreds* of children!"

The church has provided a great deal of support to these seniors in the past—however unwittingly. It would be a grave disservice to these same members if the church did not provide them with the means to remain viably connected to the life of the church.

## Consider This

Incorporating the elderly into the life of the church requires a careful examination of the nature of church ministries. Looking at several facets of church life will reveal ways that seniors have been inadvertently, but surely, marginalized or excluded from church activities.

**WORSHIP** Many churches have adopted a more contemporary style of worship. Once seniors could turn the right page in their hymnal just by hearing the name of a song, but they now find that their familiar hymnals are no longer used. Instead, they are expected to read unfamiliar lyrics from a projection screen at the front of the sanctuary or on television monitors attached to side walls. Often, their eyesight is too poor to read the lyrics, the tunes sound like music from a commercial radio station, or some degree of hearing loss may make it impossible to follow what might be a new and unfamiliar order of service. Following are some suggestions to alleviate these problems.

There has been documented a resurgence of interest in the "old" African American spirituals among young generations. Incorporate some of these favorites back into the worship service. Younger members can benefit from their time-honored messages. Seniors will feel a renewed sense of connection to the worship service.

Instead of only projecting lyrics onto a screen, for those whose sight is failing include a large-print insert in the bulletin that includes the lyrics for that Sunday's worship. Many churches install commercial assistive listening devices (ALDs) for those in the congregation who have hearing loss. There is a variety of types of systems, including radio frequency, infrared, and induction loop systems, and many different suppliers. Some companies have special prices for churches. Earlink (www.earlink.com) provides a good analysis of the different systems and the arena for which each is most effective.

**OUTREACH** Some seniors who in the past have taken an active part in church outreach ministries may suddenly find that they are no longer able—effectively or at all—what they used to accomplish with ease and delight. For instance, one widowed, self-proclaimed "active senior" used to take into her home church members who were elderly and infirm. A home-care nurse who attended the same church paid a professional visit to an infirm senior who was enjoying that  member's hospitality. The nurse called the pastor to inform him that the active senior was at risk for serious back and neck problems as she continued to try to lift to the toilet, turn over in bed, and otherwise care for her infirm guest.

Another elderly woman had, for decades, sent congratulatory cards to every married couple in the church upon the occasion of their wedding anniversary. Now in her upper-eighties, the woman could not hold a pen to write notes in the cards or address the envelopes. She felt her ministry was dead!

Active seniors whose strength is failing can be encouraged to recognize their new limitations and make adjustments. Instead of taking "infirm" seniors into their homes, a willing housemate might accommodate ambulatory seniors who can still care for themselves. Other like-minded seniors might go *to* the infirm and visit them in nursing homes and hospitals.

Seniors with a letter-writing ministry might benefit from technology workshops. Rather than laboriously writing out letters by hand, they might more easily send e-mail messages and "e-cards" to recipients who have Internet capabilities whether at home or in nursing care facilities.

**CHURCH OFFICE** Technology is an issue in more formal church settings as well. The last decade has seen phenomenal change in office technology. Tasks that once required many hours of human labor can now be accomplished in less than an hour by programming a machine. This is wonderful for office efficiency, but it leaves senior volunteers who may have performed these mundane tasks for decades feeling unneeded and perhaps even pushed out the church office door. Pastors and office managers may have even chosen to refrain from adopting certain new technologies because it would mean supplanting longtime senior volunteers.

The choice need not be one of either/or—keep the seniors *or* adopt the technological advances. Seniors can be made a part of the selection process when a decision is made to upgrade the church office. They can be a part of the excitement of trying new equipment and acknowledging how much more efficiently the office can operate. These same seniors may be trained in operating the new equipment—at least to the degree that they are comfortable and proficient in doing so.

If older workers are just not comfortable in the new office arrangement, there are still ways to incorporate them creatively into the work of the church office. They may lose the old job, but they may find a new one that serves the church even more effectively! They may serve as a greeter, welcoming visitors to the pastor's office or directing them to the coat closet. They may work in inventory, ordering supplies such as copy paper and pew pencils. There will always be odd jobs that need to be filled in the office. It takes compassion and perhaps a little creativity to ensure that seniors who have been a part of the church's office work can still successfully perform needed tasks.

**FELLOWSHIP** Some seniors have "practiced hospitality" and enjoyed fellowship with the saints for decades. Now, for reasons such as illness and infirmity, relocation of friends and relatives, change in their own living situations, and the death of friends and relatives, these same seniors find themselves unable to practice the gift they enjoy so much. These gracious elderly need not be left in the cold, unable to take part in the fellowship that has given them so much pleasure in the past. The church can easily make accommodations that will help them reenter the ring of fellowship.

Families can invite seniors to "co-host" meals with them when they entertain. These families can encourage seniors to invite a friend, a relative, or (if there is sufficient space) an entire family to share in the meal. The senior can choose to bring a dish to share or not. The important consideration is that hospitable seniors are able to be a part of the sort of active fellowship that they are no longer able to maintain for themselves.

Older members can also be encouraged to invite friends and neighbors to church meals. Instead of treating these after-church gatherings as only for those who have attended the preceding church service or program, seniors can comfortably invite guests without feeling as if they are imposing upon the church's hospitality. Such invitations might even evolve into an unobtrusive evangelistic ministry. Also, families who enjoy cooking and serving can volunteer to deliver and serve a meal to a senior and his or her invited guests. In this way, the senior can periodically be a host in comfortable home surroundings.

**CHURCH SCHOOL** More and more church school curricula are adopting the latest, most effective, and interesting teaching tools and techniques. These lessons—often interactive and fast-paced—are designed to keep the students' attention and portray the Bible as a Living Word that is truly relevant to twenty-first century life. However, senior church school teachers who are used to a more pedantic style of instruction are often put off by current methods. They may ignore the new curriculum packs altogether or, even worse, quit teaching.

The adoption of more progressive teaching methods does not automatically exclude the participation of senior teaching staff. Older teachers may be partnered with a teacher who is more comfortable with the new curriculum—and who may, in fact, be another elderly teacher! This partnership may also be more effective in managing the class and in coordinating the interactive lessons. Also, the senior may find it easier to learn by watching someone more at ease with the new methods than by trying to follow the classroom hints in curriculum packets.

Rather than singling out the elderly teachers, the church school superintendent may want to hold a series of teachers' workshops for the entire staff. These sessions can describe various teaching methods in an open and relaxed setting. Teachers can see classroom enactments that let them actually see how the techniques are designed to work. Workshops are also an excellent means of ensuring that the entire church school staff has received the same curriculum instruction and is prepared to work together to move the instructional program forward.

## A Prayer of Empowerment

*Lord,*
*Teach us to cherish and partner with those older friends that you've placed along our pathway. Help us to delight in seniors as time-bound, rare, and precious gifts with whom we have been blessed. Grant us the will, the desire, and the resolve to seek with urgency every opportunity to bathe in the afterglow and the overflow cast by their elongated shadows, which dance with among us.*
*Amen.*

# Where Do You Stand?

Each church must respond to the needs of its elderly members in ways that are representative of that congregation. First, however, the church must consider questions such as those posed below.

1. How have older members of your church had a positive impact on your life?

2. What are some of the ways seniors are currently taking part in the ministries of your church?

3. What are some of the ministries that appear to have *less* involvement of elderly members? Why?

4. What are some of the ministries that appear to have a preponderance of older members? Why?

## Models for Action

Consider how the elderly can be incorporated into ministries where they have less of a presence than in the past by implementing the following steps.

Describe the ministry.

List the barriers that appear to be keeping seniors away from that ministry.
- 
- 
- 
- 

Brainstorm ways in which these barriers can be eliminated.
- 
- 
- 
- 

If the barriers cannot be sufficiently eliminated, consider how the ministry can be changed to accommodate the input, talents, and presence of seniors.
- 
- 
- 
-

# CHAPTER 5

# The Elderly as Mentors

*Tell the older men to be temperate, serious, prudent, and
sound in faith, in love, and in endurance. Likewise,
tell the older women to be reverent in behavior, not to be
slanderers or slaves to drink; they are to teach what is good.*
—Titus 2:2-3

Most researchers in the area of human development agree that, because of the experiences of life and the socioeconomic crises that accompany aging, old age comes with an enhanced religious sense. For those who delineate stages of religious development, this period of faith is referred to as "resolute faith." Resolute faith is characterized by wisdom, defined by V. Bailey Gillespie in *The Experience of Faith* as a way of not only knowing about life, but of having tasted it deeply (Birmingham: Religious Education Press, 1988, p. 211). Having tasted both the bitterness and sweetness of life, the black elderly have a natural feel for what is genuine and life affirming. Because of this unique perspective that time alone can provide, they are ideal mentors for children, youth, and young adults.

Therefore, there is great value in having younger generations sit with our fountains of wisdom—the African American elderly. We have to allow our young people to learn or be taught afresh from these reservoirs of expertise and survival. Who should have more of a vested interest in seeing the younger generations of African Americans reach their fullest potential than older generations of

African Americans? Seniors are best prepared to share what they know and have experienced as survivors in an unfriendly environment littered with obstacles. They are the best equippers! This partnership must be implemented as a rite of passage for the young people in our churches.

What can our youth gain from these mentoring encounters? As people grow up, they engage in a critical process of taking messages from outside themselves and internalizing them to develop their own sense of who they are and what they believe. Mentoring relationships—in which a respected and accepting person walks with another in his or her process of maturing—are essential to growing into full adulthood. This author can recall the lessons from mentors of his youth in the following areas:

■ vocational and industrial arts skills

■ the value of religion and church as an integral part of one's moral compass and personal commitments

■ leadership training through participation in national conventions and youth rallies

■ the value of preparation: study, research, documentation

■ the difference between short-range and long-range goals

■ the value of discipline and discernment

## Consider This

A successful mentoring program involving the older and younger generations must include training and program development.

**TRAINING FOR THE MENTORS** Using the senior segment of the African American population in a mentoring program presents challenges and opportunities for churches. The elderly typically represent a pool of adults with decades of secular education and skilled work experience, but with little history of church school or youth ministry involvement. Training might include workshops on:

■ an overview of mentoring, its goals, and the most effective ways to nurture others
■ early childhood and adolescent emotional development
■ early childhood and adolescent physical health issues
■ an introduction to the twenty-first-century youth culture
■ specific expectations of children, youth, and young adults in the mentoring program
■ specific expectations of the mentors

**PROGRAM DEVELOPMENT** Perhaps the most important element of a successful mentoring program is an inspired and committed director, preferably one with training in children and youth issues and ideally one with experience in mentoring. A mentoring program should also include several key facets, including but not limited to those listed below: (Keep in mind that each program should be tailored to the experiences, interests, and needs of the individual mentors and young people in the program.)
■ consistent weekly sessions
■ group gatherings that include time for one-on-one interaction
■ offsite field trips and travel, such as visits to local college campuses for older teens
■ follow-up visits from a social worker or other counselor, as needed
■ workshops on parenting and adolescent issues for family members or caregivers
■ visits from guest speakers or celebrities to the church mentoring program

Mentoring programs should be further developed with an eye to the following considerations:

**1. Site Selection:** The program should, if at all possible, be on site at the church. If space constraints prevent this, then the program can be carried out at a neighborhood site. The site should be accessible, including exterior ramps for those who have difficulty with stairs and for those who use wheelchairs. Meeting spaces on floors other than the first require elevators for easy access. The furnishings on the site should be sturdy yet comfortable and there should be areas where the elderly and youth can sit apart from the large group and speak freely and privately.

2. **Topics:** Mentors and the program director should prepare for the weekly sessions ahead of time, creating their own lessons or purchasing appropriate curricula from health-focused and educational resources. Weekly topics can be selected from the following list:

- health and nutrition
- exercise
- study skills
- African American history
- career options
- vocational preparation
- lifestyles of successful people
- leadership training
- sharing of life stories from the elderly mentors

3. **Recruitment:** Mentors should be selected from the church body. They should be known to the congregation. If there are not enough seniors to serve as mentors, young people's names can be placed on a waiting list until mentors are available. In some cases, more than one young person might be assigned to an older mentor. This may work well if there are siblings in need of the companionship of a caring senior. It is always important, of course, to have flexibility in assignments. Having an informal gathering may reveal who will make good mentors and also help identify relational connections that indicate good mentor-to-youth matches.

Where can we find these fountains of experience and wisdom who have, in previous eras, served as pivotal and essential linkages for the nurture, growth, development, discipline, and guidance of African American children, youth, and young adults? We can find these elderly role models in the black church!

The black church is crucial not only for the recovery and corrective reclamation of African American children, youth, and young adults, but also for ensuring that the wisdom of our elders is treasured and not cast aside. It is the black church that can corral the resources to create and sustain a mentoring program between generations. It is the black church that can bring together the participants to make such a mentoring program happen. It is the black church that can remind its senior members that the best way to gain a new lease on life is to share their life's testimony with the generation to come.

Exhort your elder members to proclaim with the aging psalmist in Psalm 71:14-18:

But I will hope continually,
and will praise you yet more and more.
My mouth will tell of your righteous acts,
of your deeds of salvation all day long,
though their number is past my knowledge.
I will come praising the mighty deeds of the LORD God,
I will praise your righteousness, yours alone.
O God, from my youth you have taught me,
and I still proclaim your wondrous deeds.
So even to old age and gray hairs,
O God, do not forsake me,
until I proclaim your might to all the generations to come.

# Where Do You Stand?

1. List some of the mentors who helped to guide you in your youth.

2. What were some of the lessons these mentors taught you?

3. What lessons do you, personally, feel are important to impart to young people?

4. Are you a mentor to a young person? Why or why not?

# Models for Action

List the older members of your congregation whom you would like to see take part in a mentoring program at your church.

■

■

■

■

List the names of the young people in your church who would benefit from being associated with a mentor.
- 
- 
- 
- 

Describe the logistical aspects of a proposed mentoring program at your church, including but not limited to the following details:
- Program director:
- Weekly meeting dates:
- Time of meeting:
- Site location:

Create a flyer announcing the coming mentoring program at your church. What information do you consider to be essential to win over both mentors and youth?
- 
- 
- 
-

# CHAPTER 6

# Seniors as Parents of Young Children

Come, O children, listen to me; I will teach you
the fear of the LORD. —Psalm 34:11

"I never thought I'd be raising a child at the age of sixty-five," the woman exclaimed to no one in particular as she ushered the gangly youth into the line to register for the children's chess tournament. Was she a twenty-first-century Sarah, giving birth way past the standard childbearing and childrearing years? No! This salt-and-pepper-haired, neatly attired woman was one of a growing class of caregivers within African American families. She was an older person raising a young grandchild.

Fortunately, this woman was not left to raise the boy alone. Both she and her husband were healthy. Both were retired health professionals and able to comfortably provide for the youth. Yet there were certain realities they could not escape, such as,

■ Their energy and vigor were waning.

■ Their health, in all probability, would not stay robust.

■ Failing health would begin draining their finances.

■ Their income had stopped growing, but they faced the spiraling expense of childrearing.

■ Their advancing age made contingency plans for the care for their grandchild more crucial.

Despite the unexpected challenges, one could say that this couple was blessed. First of all, they were together; one person had not been left to raise the grandchild alone. Also, as retired health professionals—he had been a physician, she a surgical nurse—they had carefully planned for their retirement and were not financially devastated when they became guardians of their grandson. And being still mobile, they were able to drive to various locations and take advantage of the many enrichment activities available to their grandson.

But what if the situation were otherwise—as it is for so many older members of the African American community? What about those seniors who are widowed or divorced? What if, instead of a retirement annuity, there was only a monthly social security check? What about the person struggling to keep her diabetes from spiraling out of control or the one needing surgery to keep his glaucoma in check? What if there were no car, leaving them dependent on public transportation? The scenario suddenly becomes very bleak, and the future for the grandparent and child looks dire.

The African adage "It takes a village to raise a child" certainly is widely accepted as timeless wisdom. But where is the village for the less fortunate grandparent raising a young child? The village looks vastly different. Fear and crime have ravaged this village. A mobile society has scattered parts of this village to locations that, without a car, are out of reach.

In times such as these, the ministries of the African American church become indispensable to the elderly. The task of childrearing is daunting in the best of circumstances. Raising a child when one is in the twilight years can seem an insurmountable burden. The African American church must stand ready to offer aid and assistance. It must be a strong support system for a family unit that should not be made to stand alone. Where there is no village, the church must become one.

## Consider This

Generally in society, grandparenting represents an obvious role shift from the instrumental responsibility of earner, provider, and producer to the expressive role of cheerleader, encourager, and patient and forgiving supporter. However, through twists and turns in life, the elderly can be called upon to become primary care-givers—effectively, parents—for a grandchild or grandniece or nephew. This can happen for a number of reasons, including:

- death due to catastrophic accident
- death due to catastrophic disease such as HIV/AIDS
- death due to drug or alcohol abuse
- incapacitation due to drug and alcohol abuse
- incarceration
- abandonment

Whatever the reason, the elderly "parent" needs to be able to call upon the resources of the church. The following ministries may already be in place and functioning within a particular congregation. Or they may need to be initiated or fine-tuned in order to respond adequately to the needs of elderly parents as well as of the congregation in general. Whatever the status of the ministries, the African American church must stand ready to offer support and guidance to a rapidly growing segment of the population.

**DAYCARE** Even if the grandparent is retired, daycare is a necessity if the child is not yet enrolled in school. The grandparent may have doctor's appointments or need to schedule meetings with attorneys or insurance personnel. It may also be that the elderly caregiver may not be physically able to care for the youngster during the entire day.

If the church already has a daycare system in place, special accommodations can be made to see that the senior's child has transportation to the facility and back home. In a separate but related ministry, the church can devise a "travel" ministry that arranges rides for senior members to appointments that are not close to home. The rides can be provided via a church minibus or they can be provided via families within the church. A "ride board" can be created that allows seniors to post their various travel needs in date and time slots. Individuals and families from the congregation may then contact the appropriate senior to arrange for a pick-up time both at home and from the appointment. Transportation can also be provided for the youngster when accompanying the elderly caregiver.

**AFTER-SCHOOL PROGRAMS** More likely than not, when these grandparents (now raising grandkids) were raising their *own* children, the admonition was, "Be in the house when the streetlights come on!" Times have certainly changed. Many urban neighborhoods are dangerous to the point that kids are not allowed outside to play at all. Many times, green spaces in the neighborhood are not playgrounds but danger-zones strewn with broken glass and abandoned needles. After-school programs—once deemed a luxury—are, in truth, a necessity. They offer youngsters a safe environment in which to spend their late afternoon and evening hours. Many African American churches are taking the lead in developing and promoting their after school agendas.

These programs offer grandparents raising young children an ideal arrangement—at one location, their grandkids can receive instruction, tutoring, and social experiences that would ordinarily require them to travel, literally, hundreds of miles in the course of one month. In addition, they know that the children are in a secure, supervised setting.

A model program can be found at the Benjamin E. Mays Male Academy, a ministry of Greater Christ Baptist Church in Detroit, Michigan. The schedule of its after-school program includes classes such as:
- chess club
- science club

- Spanish club
- academic games
- step team
- tutoring
- glee club
- Tae Kwon Do
- basketball

Teachers from the academy's day program, as well as paraprofessional assistants, lead the sessions. Each class lasts one and one-half hours and meets twice a week. Each afternoon begins with the participants receiving a nutritious after-school snack.

Though an especially ideal ministry for grandparents raising youngsters, after-school programs fulfill a much needed service for all families in a congregation and the surrounding community.

**MEALS AND NUTRITION** The nutritional needs of the elderly often change as the status of their health changes. For instance, specialized meal preparation is required for such chronic illnesses as diabetes and high blood pressure. Couple those needs with trying to provide a growing child with healthy, nutritious meals on a fixed income and the grandparent is inviting frustration. A certified nutritionist can provide valuable tips on realistically combining the nutritional needs of both grandparent and child—while staying within a fixed income. A church-sponsored nutritionist or dietician, available to consult with clients even one day per month, would protect the health of the entire family.

The larger congregation might assist seniors raising children in more occasional ways. For example, younger families within the church might volunteer to host the grandparent and child for a meal once or twice a month. This would provide a much needed break for the senior, a time of fellowship for all, and can stretch the monthly food dollars of the older family.

**EMOTIONAL SUPPORT AND COUNSELING** For a grandparent, facing the daunting responsibilities of childrearing while at the same time recognizing the signs and limitations of aging can prove to be an emotional challenge. The stigma wrongly associated with counseling and psychological therapy may dissuade a senior parent from seeking the very support that he or she needs.

If a church has a counseling center already in place, parenting seniors can be gently yet firmly encouraged to avail themselves of these services before situations spiral out of control. Or a congregation can make arrangements for a social worker or psychologist to be at the church once a month specifically to address the needs of elderly parents. Issues the senior may want to discuss with the therapist include:

■ discipline and setting limits
■ stages of childhood development
■ realistic academic expectations
■ friends and peer pressure

*This is pure and undefiled religion in the sight of our God and Father, to visit orphans and widows in their distress, and to keep oneself unstained by the world.*

The book of James tells us that caring for those at both ends of the age continuum—the young and the old—is as much a mark of true faith as is keeping oneself uncontaminated by the world (1:27). How much more so is it incumbent on us to validate our religion by caring for the widow or widower who is him or herself caring for one whose parents are unavailable? And lest we forget one of the most quoted propositions of James, let us recall his admonition that faith without works is dead (2:17). The works cited above, however prosaic they may seem, reveal pure faith indeed.

## Where Do You Stand?

1. What, if any, ministries are already in place at your church that serve the needs of elderly parents?

2. What, if any, ministries are in place that serve the needs of children being raised by elderly parents?

3. List the senior members of your church who are raising young people.

4. Of the senior parents listed above, what do you know of their special needs and the needs of the children they are raising?

## Models for Action

Consider your answers in the section above and respond to the following questions.

What new ministries would best serve the elderly "parents" in your church?

■

■

■

■

How would you revise current ministries to better serve the elderly caregivers in your church?

■

■

■

■

What could you do, personally, to minister to a particular senior-headed family in your church?

# CHAPTER 7

# Practical Life Issues for the Elderly

She considers a field and buys it;
with the fruit of her hands she plants a vineyard.
—Proverbs 31:16

An episode from the biblical saga of Isaac, the son of Abraham, provides a paradigm for what one might describe as the Isaac Syndrome. In Genesis 27, Isaac, being advanced in age, had come to a point in his pilgrimage when the years had ravished the acumen of sensual perception. His vitality had waned significantly. His energy was pretty much spent. His body was bent and bowed. Isaac's senses of sight, smell, taste, and hearing had deteriorated into an irreversible state. Isaac's zest for life was rapidly approaching total depletion. He realized now, unlike at any time before, that there was an urgency to set the affairs of his legacy in order. He had to come face to face with the truth and consequences of delayed judgment. Isaac had waited too long! He was forced to face the fact that he had been manipulated. Those closest to him had conspired against him and, against his will, they had confiscated his promise and legacy.

Dependence had robbed Isaac of control and of the power of the time-honored tradition and practice of his clan. The opportunity of gifting the firstborn male offspring was never achieved. The privilege of and responsibility for passing his legacy of accumulation on to his elder son had been lost.

The delayed decisions of Isaac created the Isaac Syndrome with consequences that were irrevocable. The syndrome occurred because Isaac sought to put his affairs in order after his health had failed, his strength had waned, his vision had dimmed, and his mind had dulled. Isaac's five senses of perception had been compromised by the weight of the years of his lifelong journey. Isaac's delay in decisions of legacy transfer produced an unintended legacy of contention and strife. The Isaac saga provides an excellent lesson in learning from a negative. It is a lesson in how *not* to handle and provide for legacies!

## Consider This

Longevity blesses even the most marginalized among us. We all accumulate something of value during our lifetimes, something that we ought to consider as having some measure of lasting value as a memorial or as a legacy to be periodically observed and noted in some tangible manner. Only the decisions of the living can set in motion the guarantee of a "living legacy." Only in that way will the value of the sacrifices of a lifetime of the black elderly be honored and recognized.

Longevity has its advantages; it stockpiles valuable assets that accumulate over time. The value of a little money over a lot of time creates financial legacies. Aging African Americans must be made aware (or reminded) of their accrued value over the years of "hard labor" as instrumental achievers. Thus, built up over the years, their value requires new and more creative levels of management. Older blacks must be educated concerning estate management and assisted with the transfer of their financial legacies.

Key components of that management responsibility are addressed here, but only in a superficial way. Each deserves further research and consideration by the individuals themselves, as well as discussion with family and trusted legal and financial advisors.

**A CURRENT WILL** The literature in a personal financial planning seminar listed the "Ten Reasons to Make a Will." In that list, the authors made the following memorable observation: "Most of us live—at least part-time—in a pleasant, relaxing place called Someday Isle, 'Someday I'll get around to it.' But when it comes to making your will, it's never too soon to get started. Your will should be the centerpiece of your overall estate plan to reduce taxes and ensure that your hard-won assets are enjoyed by whom you want, in the way you want."

A last will and testament addresses and articulates your personal wishes, desires, and intentions for the disposal and distribution of your accumulated legacy in the event of death. It makes legally binding the who, what, when, where, and how of your material bequests. An updated will alleviates stress, strain, and frustration for those loved ones from whom you are separated by the ultimate reality of death.

Through a properly written and witnessed will, you can, among other things:

■ Nominate a trusted representative as executor of your estate.

■ Create a tax-saving trust for your surviving spouse.

■ Establish a trust and guardianship for minor children and grandchildren.

■ Make personal bequests of specific items or amounts.

■ Designate gifts to charity.

■ Administer out-of-state property.

**ESTATE PLANNING AND PLANNED GIVING** Estate planning involves the preservation and distribution of wealth, either before or after death. When executed in a timely fashion, estate planning may aid in achieving the following:

■ Alleviate of administrative court costs.

■ Provide for orderly distribution of assets without delay.

■ Minimize of legal fees and estate taxes.

The technical nature of estate planning requires careful coordination with the help of an estate planning attorney. An estate plan should be reviewed every two or three years to make adjustments for changes in tax laws or one's personal and financial situation.

One common aspect of estate planning is called planned giving. An individual may choose to make substantial donations to a charitable organization posthumously by including a planned giving clause in his or her will. Alternatively, a charitable endowment, trust, or annuity established late in life provides a protected stream of income during life, simultaneously taking advantage of significant tax advantages without eroding one's accumulated financial legacy. Such planned giving offers several advantages:

- generates an income-tax deduction
- increases and diversifies one's income
- avoids the payment of a capital gains tax on highly appreciated and low yielding assets (such as stocks or real estate)
- eliminates asset management problems
- reduces estate taxes
- avoids probate costs
- assists one's favorite charity, institution, or organization

A certified personal financial planner (CFP)—ideally one retained by the church as a vital part of its *pro bono* legal ministry—can provide illustrations of such instruments. A worthy CPF, in concert with a church's *pro bono* ministry (see below), can simplify the technical and make it understandable for older African Americans.

**PRO BONO LEGAL SERVICES** *Pro bono* legal services are provided by a legal professional without compensation from the client. Many African American congregations have attorneys among their members. Their talents need to be organized into a ministry that serves the interests of the black elderly. Such a *pro bono* ministry is low budget, but the potential is empowering and legacy sustaining.

This ministry might offer private consultations with seniors who want to draft a will or discuss estate planning. It might also sponsor seminars or workshops that educate older members as to options. All such services must be confidential, of course, and the church leadership should be accountable for appointing legal professionals with the appropriate credentials—and personal integrity.

**WHO WILL CHOOSE FOR YOU?** There is a variety of legal tools at our disposal that give us the ability to decide *now* who will make decisions on our behalf in the future. The ability to choose today who will make critical life decisions tomorrow or in years to come can be a source of comfort and security, both for the person choosing now and those who will be confronted with difficult choices later.

A *power of attorney* grants the privilege of decision-making in the interest of a person who may become incapacitated because of age, accident, failing health, or other restrictive challenges. This power of attorney may be "durable" (applying to a variety of circumstances over time) or "limited" (governing only specific decisions or a particular time frame).

In the event of a life and death situation, a *living will* makes clear the wishes of a person if and when it has been determined that one's physical and mental state and condition are irreversible and any quality of life is non-existent. A living will makes clear in a written document the desire not to be sustained by artificial and mechanical life-support apparatus.

A *living trust* allows one to manage one's wealth while alive and provides for a trustee of that wealth should that individual become incapacitated. Under a living trust, the person's assets avoid probate, which in some states can be costly and time consuming, allowing assets to be distributed quickly upon the death of the owner. Such trusts are difficult to contest in court, so they avert many family squabbles. A trust also provides for privacy regarding the size of one's estate and the distribution of one's wealth.

## "With Long Life I Will Satisfy Them"

The African American church must enlarge the vision of its mission and ministries in a commitment to preserve and memorialize the life pilgrimage, sacrifices, and contributions of members of long standing. Aging blacks must be made aware of their accrued worth and value and then taught how to preserve that legacy. By making decisions now, they can avoid the erosion or misappropriation of their hard-earned resources. Consultation with spouse, children, family members, friends, and trusted financial and legal professionals can ease the transition when that time comes for "God to call and you to answer." Thoughtful planning provides one's survivors the opportunity to move toward grief resolution with "sacred memories." As part and parcel of these ministries of the African American church, the Isaac Syndrome can be significantly remedied.

The Isaac Syndrome is a process of delay and postponement. It is a stunted period of monumental consequences. It is a season of delayed decisions of critical importance. This decline is the consequence of advancing years and postponed execution. The capacity to see, smell, hear, taste, or feel will have waxed and waned. If and when the Isaac Syndrome is allowed to set in, the will and wishes of older persons are compromised!

The Isaac Syndrome can and does take place when a person delays making arrangements for realizing, recognizing, and executing responsibility for the timely protection and transfer of his or her earthly accumulations. Failure to make arrangements for transfers in a decent and orderly manner—and according to a person's own desires and wishes—can blot out one's contributions and legacy.

The Isaac Syndrome is identified and presented to remind the black elderly and the African American church that older members of the congregation are all worth more than is realized. In both a spiritual and a material sense, older African Americans are worth far more than anyone may recognize. The black church must become more intentional about teaching its older members to recognize their accumulated wealth and to manage the transfer of their financial legacies. This must become an integral part of the mission and ministries of the black church in the twenty-first century.

## Where Do You Stand?

1. What experience have you had with loved ones who passed without making adequate preparation for the transfer or distribution or their personal and material legacy?

2. What do you consider to be your legacy?

3. What arrangements have you made to pass on this legacy?

4. What resources, if any, does your church offer to assist its members in making plans for the transfer of personal and material legacies?

## Models for Action

This chapter discussed a variety of fairly complicated options with significant legal implications, all related to the death and dying of an individual. How might you or your church approach the advisability and necessity of considering these options and implementing them in the individual lives of your older (and younger) members? Consider the list below:

■ a current last will and testament

- power of attorney
- living wills and trusts
- estate planning
- planned giving
- long-term-care insurance coverage
- non-taxable transfer of real estate
- funeral arrangements
- a *pro bono* legal ministry

# CHAPTER 8

# Ministries of Caring

...but the members may have the same care for one another.
—1 Corinthians 12:25

African American churches, whether they are large or small, urban, suburban, or rural, respond to the demographics of their congregations. However, the rapid graying of society may not be as apparent as other markers, and its effect on the church may, therefore, come upon the church's leadership suddenly. For example, a congregation with a median age of 55 may be surrounded by a community with a youthful population of young families with many children. In contrast, a church that draws the younger generation may be located in a neighborhood that hosts one or more assisted-living or senior residences. Such realities inform—or ought to inform—the direction of the mission and the ministries of a church to its elderly population.

Whether the church's congregation is comprised primarily of aging members or not, many different models of ministry can be adapted to fit the needs of a particular congregation and its surrounding community. The ministry models described below are by no means comprehensive or exhaustive. Rather, they represent but a small sampling of the many congregations that are serving seniors in innovative and compassionate ways. They represent churches from many major sections of the United States. Examine these descriptions, and then actively seek out additional models in your own locale to study and use as a springboard to create new models or fine tune already existing ministries for the elderly.

## Consider This

**Greater Christ Baptist Church, Detroit, Michigan** Believing that the church has a responsibility to serve both the temporal as well as the spiritual needs of the surrounding community, the Rev. Dr. James C. Perkins has established numerous enterprises that support that vision, including the Fellowship Nonprofit Housing Corporation and the Benjamin E. Mays Male Academy. As the author of *Building Up Zion's Walls: Ministry for Empowering the African American Family* (Judson Press, 1999), Dr. Perkins has made it his mission to establish ministries that not only can serve nuclear and extended families but that can also function as models for the benefit of other congregations. The Senior Citizens Ministry Commission (the Commission) of Greater Christ Baptist Church is an outgrowth of that vision.

Succinctly stated, the purpose of the Commission is "to develop a ministry to meet the needs of the senior members of our congregation." The Commission is made up of all members of Greater Christ Baptist Church who are interested in senior citizens as a focus in ministry. The Commission meets once each month.

In order to make the Commission a vital part of the church's congregational life, the entire month of May is designated Senior Emphasis Month. During this month, the church makes a more concentrated effort to make all members aware of the senior citizen ministries.

Following are brief descriptions of each senior ministry sponsored by the Commission.

*Adopt-A-Senior Program*: This program encourages younger members to adopt a senior within the church to look after and assist in any way possible. Their commitment includes making daily telephone calls to alleviate loneliness, remembering birthdays, running errands, providing transportation, and helping out with minor home repair projects.

*Legal Referral Service*: This service provides free legal counsel to seniors within the church and in the surrounding community. It is sponsored in cooperation with the Wayne County Legal Aid Society and is available on the second Monday of each month.

*Senior Citizens Emphasis Day*: This annual day in the church is set aside specifically to thank God for the aging process and to highlight the talents and contributions of the senior saints.

*Share-A-Home*: This program connects home providers with home seekers for the mutual benefit of each. It seeks to facilitate suitable matches for seniors looking to share living space.

*Senior Connector*: This program provides referrals to seniors for the following services (and others as needed): home evaluation, transportation, "Meals on Wheels," housekeeping, home repairs, telephone reassurance.

**The Monumental Baptist Church, Jersey City, New Jersey** The late Reverend Ercel F. Webb was a dynamic and energetic visionary who transformed the environment of his church and the surrounding area in amazing ways. Some of the ministries include a Saturday food pantry, the adoption and sponsorship of libraries at public and parochial schools, and the purchase and renovation of abandoned apartment buildings near the church.

Because his vision was embedded within his congregation, the Monumental Elderly Ministry is vibrant and comprehensive to this day. One primary component of this ministry is the renovated apartments located near the church, called Homes of the Saints. Elderly members (usually women) live rent-free in these apartments. At the Saturday morning food pantry and clothing closet distribution centers, senior citizens receive priority attention.

The congregation's desire to honor its senior members is reflected in another concrete way. Twice annually, before Thanksgiving and again prior to the Christmas holiday, every Monumental Church member age sixty-five or older with twenty-five years of membership in the church is provided with a check to use as they see fit. This gift is a way of showing appreciation and respect for these members.

**Concord Baptist Church of Christ, Brooklyn, New York** The Concord Baptist Church of Christ has a distinguished history of creative response to the needs and dignity of African Americans. The mission and ministries of the Concord congregation have been comprehensive in scope and influence. The Concord Nursing Home, Inc., was founded in 1975. This 122-bed facility was expanded in 2003 as the Concord Nursing and Rehabilitation Center. Residents live in attractive and comfortable private and semi-private rooms. There are expansive dining rooms on each floor. The center provides an Adult Day Health Care Center, a seventeen-bed ventilator unit, rehabilitation services, certified social workers, dieticians, recreational therapists, onsite beauticians and barbers, and pastoral services.

Several apartment buildings have been purchased and renovated next to the church that provide affordable housing for elderly members as well as for the community at large.

In addition, the church has continued its practice and tradition of feeding seniors on select Sundays following morning worship and providing them with transportation.

**Lewis Chapel Missionary Baptist Church, Fayetteville, North Carolina** With both a mission and commitment to reach the masses for Christ, the ministries of the Lewis Chapel congregation are comprehensive. The John D. Fuller Place, constructed in 1976, is a 47-unit senior citizen apartment complex that provides housing for older members of the congregation and community. The Senior

Citizen's Noonday Prayer Service and Bible Study meets weekly on Wednesdays. Lunch and transportation are provided.

The church van picks up all residents of the John D. Fuller Place Community. An "Intergeneration Academy" meets on Saturdays. The young adult ministry provides services for elderly members, such as housecleaning and lawn care. The youth, with the help of their parents, prepare occasional meals for seniors. Meals are also provided by the women's ministry, the Boy Scouts and Girl Scouts, individual congregants, and many other ministries of the church.

**West Hunter Street Baptist Church, Atlanta, Georgia** In 1985, the five-story, 100-unit Ralph David Abernathy Towers was constructed. It is located on what was formerly a part of the church's parking lot (plus the purchase of two additional lots). The facility provides housing for the elderly, the handicapped, and people with disabilities. The support services and ministries include the providing of medical literature, workshops on diabetes, blood pressure screenings, diet and nutrition counseling, and exercise programs.

The Towers also provides support services, informational services, a companion program, a nurses aide service, "Meals on Wheels," and weekly deliveries of fresh fruit and freshly baked breads.

**Friendship Baptist Church, Charlotte, North Carolina** As a church with multiple pastors serving on its staff, Friendship Baptist has enjoyed the specialized leadership of a minister of seniors. (Currently, a retired pastor from Buffalo, New York, serves in that position.)

The church also sponsors a program that meets monthly with seniors to address issues affecting the healthcare and finances of older citizens. Issues such as budgeting, banking, financial planning, and making funeral arrangements are discussed.

**Pinn Memorial Baptist Church, Philadelphia, Pennsylvania** In addition to its senior citizen apartment complex, Pinn Memorial operates an intergenerational program related to schools in the area. Schoolchildren interview seniors and then write a paper from the contents of the interviews. Children maintain contact with their seniors as adopted grandparents.

**Providence Baptist Church, Baltimore, Maryland** In 1993, Rev. Marcus G. Wood, who served as pastor of Providence Baptist for fifty years, proposed to the congregation the construction of a Medical Adult Day Care Center. Four years later, this facility opened with a capacity to accommodate fifty adults. By design, a registered nurse is required to be on duty at all times. Because the socioeconomic, income, and health status of approximately twenty-five widows do not render them eligible for the Medical Adult Day Care Center, there is a Golden Gleaners Club as an additional ministry for senior citizens.

In addition, children and youth interview the elderly about their lifestyles as a means of enriching the lives of the church's youth, especially concerning the educational experiences, living conditions, discipline, and other details of seniors' lives.

**Second Baptist Church, Los Angeles, California** The Second Baptist Church model for mission and ministry with senior adults is best described as a comprehensive, integrated ministry. It has enjoyed the direction and coordination of a specialized social services coordinator who is employed for twelve hours per week on Mondays and Wednesdays. The position of "senior services coordinator" was changed to "social services coordinator" to allow for an expanded ministry that provides for the service needs not only of all church members but of community members as well. However, services to seniors remain the primary and major focus of the ministry. The coordinator networks with other senior adult programs in the community, programs sponsored by three sister congregations.

# Where Do You Stand?

Consider the following story from the earliest days of the Christian church and then respond to the questions that follow.

> *Now at this time while the disciples were increasing in number, a complaint arose on the part of the Hellenistic Jews against the native Hebrews, because their widows were being overlooked in the daily serving of food. And the twelve summoned the congregation of the disciples and said, "It is not desirable for us to neglect the word of God in order to serve tables. But select among you, seven men of good reputation, full of the Spirit and of wisdom who may take charge of this task. (Acts 6:1–3)*

1. Whose responsibility is caring for the elderly?

2. In what ways does caring for the elderly help members of the congregation fulfill their responsibilities as Christians?

3. What ministries to the elderly are most needed in your congregation?

4. Of the models for ministry presented in this chapter, which ones could best be adapted for your congregation? Why?

5. What components do you think are necessary for a successful ministry to seniors?

## Models for Action

For each ministry to the elderly listed in your answers above, provide the following information based upon your own congregation.

1. [Name of Ministry]
- Ministry chair
- Ministry members
- Seniors to be served
- Expected results
- Timetable for expected results

2. [Name of Ministry]
- Ministry chair
- Ministry members
- Seniors to be served
- Expected results
- Timetable for expected results

3. [Name of Ministry]
- Ministry chair
- Ministry members

- Seniors to be served
- Expected results
- Timetable for expected results

4. [Name of Ministry]
- Ministry chair
- Ministry members
- Seniors to be served
- Expected results
- Timetable for expected results

5. [Name of Ministry]
- Ministry chair
- Ministry members
- Seniors to be served
- Expected results
- Timetable for expected results

# CHAPTER 9

# The Elderly Pastor

So even to old age and gray hairs, O God, do not forsake me,
until I proclaim your might to all the generations to come.
—Psalm 71:18

It has been observed that in every stage of human transition, we are educated, coached, and even prepped for the next new phase of our journey. Aging and old age are the exception to this rule. There is neither coaching nor practical preparation for growing old. It is biologically, nutritionally, socially, economically, psychologically, emotionally, and medically thrust upon us. We are left to adjust as best we can! In that respect, the circumstances surrounding the retirement of an elderly pastor are no different.

The African American community has benefited greatly from the visionary leadership, creative commitment, and political advocacy of the black church. Its sense of sociopolitical activity has been the direct result of the courage and valor of its pastoral leadership. That leadership range has been both broad and diverse. A very small sampling would include the likes of George Liele, Richard Allen, and Henry McNeil Turner, as well as Adam Clayton Powell Jr., Gardner C. Taylor, Claude Black, Martin Luther King Jr., Carolyn Tyler Guidry, and Renita J. Weems. For the most part, that pastoral leadership has concerned itself with rescuing, liberating, delivering, protecting, defending, training, preparing, educating, encouraging, building, and promoting the dreams and aspirations of African Americans. The fruits resulting from the labor of this broad range of leaders have both sustained and empowered a multitude of generations. Without the assertive and confident leadership provided by our visionary pastors, progress among African Americans would have been measurably restricted, if not radically altered. The combination of meager resources and mighty "sweat equity" became the foundation of black progress. Under the auspices of black churches and religiously influenced fraternal organizations, great institutions of service have been constructed. Yet, too few have been maintained. How and why does this happen?

Too frequently, pastors who have built great institutional enterprises prolong their leadership stays well beyond their years of managerial strength and vitality only to find themselves presiding over the decay of what they have helped to build. Accomplishments resulting from sustained periods of creative and visionary leadership tumble down around them. Because leadership transition is left to chance, these crumbling institutions are inherited by inept or unprepared successors who are elevated by default. Sadly, models of leadership transition and replacement that preserve a legacy of accomplishments are too rarely embraced and implemented.

For a pastor, considerations of retirement may prompt the recognition that one's pastoral leadership has focused on maintenance rather than discipling. Such a realization can be so disturbing that it precludes the raising of critical and pivotal questions about the type of new leadership essential for the continued well-being of the congregation.

Determining when to retire as pastor brings to the forefront a situation peculiar to that ministry. By both responsibility and expectations, a pastor encompasses sustained and comprehensive relationships with the congregation. These relationships are modeled by Jesus in his parable of the Good Shepherd (John 10:1-18). The term *pastor* implies the existence of multigenerational and intergenerational relationships between shepherd and flock. These relationships encompass a connection that spans the total spectrum of human transactions, literally from the cradle to the grave. These connections are not easily untangled and rearranged upon the occasion of retirement. The minister must appreciate that retirement is from a career as a pastor—not from a lifetime call to service. So, when contemplating pastoral retirement, the following questions must be addressed by the pastor and congregation:

■ What preparations have been made for the continued survival, growth, development, and implementation of the vision for the congregation?

■ What should be done as far as leadership replacement and transition?

■ What is the best way to divest a pastor of a tenure of leadership?

There are several patterns for pastoral leadership transition that have proven successful:

1. Identify a young ministerial staff person serving with a pastoral focus. Gradually, in stages, give that person increased responsibilities and training in the mission and ministries of the church and congregation.

2. In a church with a full ministerial staff, rotate staff positions and responsibilities over time. This strategy allows the congregation to observe, work with, and recognize potential ministerial or pastoral skills and gifts of leadership.

3. Initiate contact and conversation with theological schools and seminaries, asking them to identify and recommend possible candidates as pastoral assistants or successors.

4. Some denominations provide specialized databases with search and match capabilities that are helpful in the pastoral placement process.

## Consider This

Dr. George E. Weaver has described the plight of too large a percentage of pastoral leadership in African American churches: "Too old to pastor, too broke to quit." How sad a commentary, if indeed it is true.

In a great many situations, because congregations have made no provisions for their minister's survival during retirement, black churches have suffered from leadership that is no longer effective. This problem is not necessarily the result of the stubborn resistance of the incumbent pastor, as some congregations would have you believe. "The truth of the matter," the late Dr. Samuel De Witt Proctor asserted, "is that too few black churches prepare a comfortable retirement benefit plan or a means of dignified exit for their pastoral leadership." In fact, it is not unusual for church lay leaders to inquire about the planning and preparation of retirement benefits as an afterthought or in the time of a crisis. Sad to admit, the only plan in the majority of black churches is for the minister to die in the pulpit!

When it comes down to arranging the timing for pastoral retirement, that transition involves careful consideration of the following pivotal issues:

■ Has the pastor been adequately supported financially by the congregation?

■ Has the pastor, in partnership with the congregation, thoughtfully planned for and managed the financial aspects of retirement?

The challenge on the part of pastors, church officers, and congregations is to provide benefit packages of security and protection for the pastor that are comprehensive in coverage. Congregations have a responsibility and obligation to provide protection for the leaders who serve us by what amounts to being "on call" almost constantly. Comprehensive coverage, for pastors and their families, ought to include the following:

■ medical insurance

■ dental coverage

■ disability insurance

■ survivor death benefits

■ a retirement annuity that is instantly vested, portable, and member owned and directed

One of the travesties in some congregations has been the investment in "key person" policies during times of new construction or expansion. Although these policies protect the officers of the church in the case of the death or disability of the pastor, the average member in the pew is often given the impression that, in the time of a crisis or in the event of the disability or death of the pastor, all is well and in order for the pastor and/or the pastor's family. That is far from the case with policies designed to protect the church and its officers from financial liability.

Comprehensive benefits packages, on the other hand, enable both ministers and churches to live in dignity and to separate in love and fondness. The Ministers and Missionaries Benefit Board (MMBB) of the American Baptist Churches, Inc., represents one of the very best benefit plans for the protection of pastors and church employees. In existence since 1911, this compassionate ministry has had a much felt and much appreciated presence in the lives of countless pastors and their dependents. MMBB has entered into partnership with the Progressive National Baptist Convention, National Baptist Convention USA, and National Baptist Convention of America to design affiliate retirement plans for benefit protection and security. These benefits support and sustain pastoral families with dignity and confidentiality in times of transition, accident, crisis, emergency, and death.

## Straining Forward to What Lies Ahead

The ability to leave what was and look forward to what is yet to unfold represents a psychologically sound frame of mind. One need not take on *all* of Paul's exhortation to "forget what lies behind" (see Philippians 3:13-14); there are many memories to be cherished and relationships to be preserved when a pastor retires. However, the ability to embrace the future with confidence, not with regrets or resentment, is a retirement gift beyond all others.

Who best models this principle of "straining forward to what is ahead" than the well-adjusted, retired minister who possesses a wealth of experience that is needed in many church settings beyond the congregational position that has just been vacated? There can be renewal in new and different fields of service. Retirement security and protected benefits coupled with Social Security benefits and personal savings not only make for an exit strategy on the road to pastoral retirement, but for opportunities for continued creative ministry. As a less demanding but equally fulfilling vocation, experienced and seasoned ministers are thereby available to serve other churches as interim ministers and to provide pastoral leadership in a time when congregations experience leadership transitions and vacancies.

## Where Do You Stand?

1. Pastors, regardless of your age, how have your gifts evolved throughout your ministry?

2. Pastors, how do you envision your ministry role when you retire?

3. Congregations, under what circumstances do you envision your pastor retiring?

4. Congregations, what preparations have you made toward your pastor's retirement?

# Models for Action

Consider the following real-life models for pastoral transition, and evaluate the advantages of each strategy. Which model might work most effectively in your congregation? Why?

### John J. Rector–E. Thurman Walker Model

**Antioch Baptist Church, San Antonio, Texas** Dr. John J. Rector, a second-generation pastor, was a gifted preacher, a compassionate minister, and a master builder and developer of both the congregation and the physical building of the Antioch Baptist Church. For the last years of his life, he lived with health challenges, challenges that he recognized and for which he began to make provision as he acknowledged his waning strength.

In the summer of 1986, Dr. Rector invited a young seminarian named E. Thurman Walker to work with his youth ministry. In 1987, Dr. Rector offered that seminarian full-time employment. After his seminary graduation, Pastor Walker worked as youth pastor for Antioch Baptist Church for two and a half years. In 1991, he was named copastor of the congregation.

Prior to Dr. Rector's death, the church conducted a vote to determine whether Pastor Walker would become its next pastor. The congregation approved his selection, and the Rev. E. Thurman Walker has served as pastor of the Antioch Church since 1993.

### Samuel DeWitt Proctor–Calvin O. Butts III Model

**Abyssinian Baptist Church, Harlem, New York** The late Dr. Samuel Proctor served the Abyssinian Baptist Church as senior pastor for seventeen years. There were several other ministers also employed by the congregation during Dr. Proctor's tenure. One of these ministers, Calvin O. Butts III, started at the church as a seminarian and continued in ministerial service following his graduation.

Dr. Proctor announced his intended retirement to the officers of the church in June 1988, to become effective one year later on June 30, 1989. This announcement provided the officers and the congregation time and opportunity to make arrangements for its future leadership. Dr. Butts was elected pastor; he has now served as senior pastor for more than fourteen years.

### Gardner C. Taylor – Gary V. Simpson Model

**Concord Baptist Church of Christ, Brooklyn, New York** After forty-two years as pastor of the Concord Baptist Church of Christ in Brooklyn, New York, Dr. Gardner C. Taylor retired as pastor. He announced his retirement plans in December 1989, to become effective June 1990. Upon receiving this announcement, the church officers and congregation asked Dr. Taylor to guide them through the process of electing a new pastor.

In anticipation of his approaching retirement, Dr. Taylor took two critical steps. First, he led the officers and congregation in the design of an additional compensation package for the future pastor, including retirement benefits. Second, he had invited a wide variety of guest preachers to the Concord Church pulpit as a means of providing exposure for the congregation. The congregation was given the opportunity to consider three final candidates. Two of the three candidates had served on the pastoral staff of Concord Church. Dr. Gary Simpson, by vote of the Concord congregation, was called as pastor at the church he had served for more than twelve years.

### Harry Wright – Lawrence Everett Akers III Model

**Cornerstone Baptist Church, Brooklyn, New York** After twenty-one years as pastor of the Cornerstone Baptist Church in Brooklyn, New York, Dr. Harry Wright retired. He did so after orchestrating what appears at the outset to be a seamless transition of ministerial leadership. While this transition has only recently taken place, the thoughtful planning and anticipation provide a model worthy of emulation.

At the age of sixty-nine, Dr. Wright started to think about retirement, not motivated by pressure, health challenges, or affordability but by reflection on the future ministry of Cornerstone Church. He thought about this for more than two years and described it as his attempt to spare the congregation the experience of "transitional trauma." During this time, Dr. Wright sought to discern the kind of leadership the church might need and from which it might profit for at least the next twenty ears. He reflected on five areas: pastoral warmth, a vision for the new era, the need for youthfulness and zest, the desire for a scholarly preacher, and the necessity of administrative gifts and skills.

Over the years of his tenure, Dr. Wright had invited young ministers to serve as guest preachers, as summer interns, and in other capacities on other occasions. He had observed these visiting ministers carefully and prayerfully. Then, after sharing the date of his retirement, Dr. Wright called the church together and offered to name a successor if the congregation was willing to entertain a change in the provisions of the by-laws. After the congregation voted to waive the usual pastoral leadership search process, Dr. Wright recommended the young man who had served as his assistant for more than four years. The Reverend Lawrence Akers III was chosen as pastor-elect, and Cornerstone never experienced a gap in ministerial leadership.

### George Weaver–Mack King Carter Model

**The Mount Olive Baptist Church, Fort Lauderdale, Florida** After a twenty-year pastorate and the construction of a church, Dr. George Weaver began talking with several persons about his plans to retire. Anticipating that goal, he initiated the construction of a retirement home in his native state of South Carolina. Over several years he shared his intention to make this transition and spoke with ministers and educators concerning his need for a ministerial colleague who might be considered as his successor.

In August, 1981, Dr. Weaver invited Dr. Mack King Carter to join him as co-pastor. After serving for almost a year and a half together as co-pastors, Dr. Weaver announced his retirement date. On the first Sunday in June 1982, Dr. Weaver preached both sermons, announced that he had resigned, and requested that the members return on the following evening for the sole purpose of voting on whether or not Dr. Carter would succeed him as pastor. Over 900 members attended that focused meeting and Mack King Carter was elected and designated "pastor-elect."

During the interim, both ministers proceeded with the understanding that the pastor-elect *was* the acting pastor. Dr. George Weaver preached his final sermon as pastor of the Mount Olive Baptist Church on the fourth Sunday in November 1982, and *immediately* departed for his home in South Carolina. The congregation's decision has endured for more than 20 years! The congregation has grown as its mission and ministries have evolved and expanded, and the ministerial staff has grown accordingly.

### Elliot J. Mason Sr.–Dumas A. Harshaw, Jr. Model

**Trinity Baptist Church, Los Angeles, California** After serving the Trinity Baptist Church congregation for 26 years, Dr. Elliott J. Mason retired as pastor on March 31, 1985 but remained in the membership. For four and a half years prior to his retirement, Dr. Mason had enjoyed the collegial partnership of assistant pastor, the Reverend Dumas A. Harshaw Jr. In preparation for his retirement, he announced his plans a year ahead of time and requested that the Trinity Church family join him in a "retirement vigil" of a six-week period of prayer. Dr. Mason's desire was to seek the work of the Holy Spirit to break the ties of longevity.

The Reverend Harshaw Jr. was elected pastor of Trinity one month to the date of Dr. Mason's date of retirement from the pastorate of Trinity Baptist Church. Dr. Mason led the congregation through the process of electing the new pastor—a process that included arranging for compensation and retirement benefits. Dr. Mason stipulated that, while he and Mrs. Geraldine P. Mason would maintain their membership, he would not officiate at funerals, but would, at the pastor's request, on *some* occasions offer a few remarks! With this understanding, Dr. Mason participated in the installation service and occasionally agreed to preach for the pastor's anniversary. The Elliott J. Masons had harbored an abiding desire to dedicate themselves to a ministry of prayer and encouragement and thus went on to serve as co-directors of World Renewal Ministries, providing a model of ministry following a lengthy pastorate.

### Claude W. Black–Kenneth Allen Model

**Mount Zion First Baptist Church, San Antonio, Texas** Dr. Claude W. Black Jr., served as pastor of Mount Zion First Baptist Church of San Antonio for forty-nine years. Retiring in 1999, he had actually announced his intention to retire five years before, but delayed it in response to financial challenges related to a church-sponsored day care program and in the interests of needed renewal in the church structure. Announcing his definitive retirement intent a year prior, Dr. Black began the process of developing the pastoral search committee, which meant preparing a pastoral budget and package. According to Dr. Black, a disadvantage of a long pastoral tenure is that the congregation has little concept of the expense and cost of securing new pastoral leadership. Further, he says he had to recognize that as the search committee process became more informed, it also became more political, so he had to recognize the politics of calling a minister as his successor, acknowledge that committee members were working for their interests, and be aware of how relationships influenced the process. He warns against retiring pastors over-using their influence. In the end, the

Reverend Kenneth Allen joined the ministerial staff three years prior to his election as pastor.

Dr. Black indicates that there were points when he thought it was time to go, yet others thought he should stay. He admonishes pastors to realize that the attitudes of congregations change and there will always be some people who want you to stay and others who are just waiting for you to go.

### Marcus G. Wood–Douglas Sommers Model

**Providence Baptist Church, Baltimore, Maryland** After more than fifty years as pastor of the Providence Baptist Church of Baltimore, the Reverend Marcus Wood is still blessed with the ability to do active ministry. Until recently, he drove a VW "Bug" and not long ago, he led the congregation in the construction of a Senior Day Care facility and the addition of an educational wing.

In order to facilitate the leadership transition of the Providence Church, Pastor Wood led the congregation in identifying and calling the Reverend Douglas Sommers as co-pastor. Pastor Wood aided the congregation in entering such an arrangement by recommending that his own compensation/pastoral budget be transferred to the pool of resources that would enable the church to negotiate with the new co-pastor. He began his retirement with income provided by his denominational retirement plan and an annual salary of one dollar. Pastor Sommers came on board and has assumed most of the preaching responsibility and other pastoral duties.

### Elmer L. Fowler–Allan V. Ragland Model

**Third Baptist Church, Chicago, Illinois** The Reverend Elmer L. Fowler served as the organizing pastor of the Third Baptist Church for nearly thirty years. He announced his retirement in the spring of 1992 and agreed to shepherd the congregation through the search process. Pastor Fowler, a member of the Progressive National

Baptist Convention, Inc., (PNBC), sought the counsel and recommendations of conventional confidants, three of whom were former presidents of PNBC. Pastor Fowler followed up on recommendations and had an initial telephone conversation with Dr. Allan V. Ragland. That telephone conversation was followed by an invitation for a weekend visit to preach, which, in turn, was followed by a second invitation to bring his family, preach, and have a meeting with a group of officers, department chairs, and church members, during which Reverend Fowler was present, but silent!

The church had voted unanimously to elect Dr. Ragland as its next pastor, and after prayerful consideration, Dr. Ragland agreed to accept the Third Baptist Congregation's call to serve as its new minister. He was elected pastor in November, 1992 and installed in April of 1993.

Pastor Fowler, who formally retired in December, 1992 led the church in the design, development, and proposal of a pastoral budget to consummate the call of the new minister, taking into consideration the realistic needs of a young pastor with a family. As closure for ministerial leadership, Pastor Fowler requested, arranged, and organized a week-long transitional revival. He was bestowed the title of Pastor Emeritus, and since he was not enrolled in a comprehensive retirement benefits plan, the church provided a monthly stipend for him. The pastors met occasionally after the transition and arrangements were made for Pastor Fowler to preach annually on the anniversary of his retirement, an invitation he accepted for two years.

CHAPTER 10

# Tell Us Your Story

And no one after drinking old wine desires new wine,
but says, "The old is good." —Luke 5:39

Oral tradition and storytelling are integral to how humanity marks
its historical turning points. Before one word of the Bible was written down, the truths we now read were passed from generation to
generation by the carriers of a sacred oral tradition. This phenom-
enon is also true in African American heritage. African villages had
sages whose sole job it was to commit to memory the history of
their ancestors. These repositories of communal wisdom were
known as *griots*. Even in twenty-first-century America, the importance of story has not diminished. At the dedication of his presi-
dential library in 2004, former President Bill Clinton shared this
sentiment with the dignitaries, family, and friends in attendance:

> I grew up in the pretelevision age, in a family of uneducated
> but smart, hard-working, caring storytellers. They taught me
> that everyone has a story. And that made politics intensely
> personal to me. It was about giving people better stories.

The life stories of aging blacks are essential for racial survival,
deliverance, liberation, empowerment, and recovery. Their living
legacies will bestow pride and dignity to all ages and segments of
the African American population. These tales are linked to the
reservoirs of accumulated wisdom. Their life stories are precious

nuggets of pure gold—and these golden nuggets are essential to the survival of African Americans. We must mine them through the means of storytelling. The goal must be to record and preserve data solicited by the "oral tradition."

These golden nuggets are also the bedrock for black Christian education. The content gleaned from the lives of our African American elders must be taught to the younger generations. The payoff for the personal and corporate existence of the race is this: If African Americans of all ages give heed to and serve the black elderly, we can save ourselves and all trailing generations. Without this essential partnership, the future is destined to be bleak.

The aim is to foster a context where younger African Americans can petition seniors to tell their life stories. We must create an environment that encourages not only curiosity but respectful listening as well. We must also educate black children and youth in the tools needed to preserve our oral traditions. We need to equip them with pen and paper, computers and cameras, trained and attentive ears and eyes, interview techniques and skills, and all of the latest in digital technology to guarantee the preservation of oral data. The technical knowledge of our young people needs to be applied in this ministry of preservation. A model of black religious education must be construed to link the practice of instant gratification with the reality that the black elderly are a time-bound commodity that is in limited supply. Our elders are indeed *limited editions!* A partnership between these age groups will serve all involved. The yield can prove effective.

## Consider This

The implementation of a storytelling model must be built upon a multi-tiered foundation. These tiers include setting, interview technique, topic, and presentation and preservation.

## Setting

The first step in this foundation is the *setting*. Provision must be made to create a setting (or environment) that allows younger and older participants to embrace, engage, encounter, and encourage one another. These encounters can take place in a number of venues, including:

■ at the senior's home or hospital room

■ during a designated youth group meeting

■ during prearranged church school sessions, involving select age groups or the entire church school body

■ during small groups that meet midweek at various members' homes

■ during a church anniversary, picnic, or other churchwide event

During any of the above gatherings, the stories can be shared in a variety of ways. It might take the format of an interview. This can be a one-to-one interview, or the senior member can be questioned in front of a group, large or small. A senior presenter might also share in front of a group where he or she can speak in response to previously submitted questions, according to a specific program theme, based upon personal preference of topics, or solely according to individual recollection and stream of consciousness.

The types of stories shared and the venues in which they are shared also depend upon the individual senior. Some may have sharp, vibrant memories, and any topic could unleash a floodgate of anecdotes. Others may have only halting memories and will need patient listeners armed with carefully worded, gently coaxing questions. In all cases, sensitivity must be exercised to protect the elderly members' dignity and self-esteem. These encounters should at all times be enjoyable for the older members and edifying for the younger participants.

**INTERVIEW TECHNIQUES** *Interviewing techniques* can vary. As alluded to previously, the encounters can be the very traditional one-on-

one interview model, with the younger interviewer taking notes or with the senior speaking into a recording device. This approach is probably best for aging members whose physical or mental health does not permit lengthy sessions or formal public presentations. (For example, a senior with arthritic knees may not be able to stand in front of a panel or congregation, and someone who has developed dementia may be confused or frightened by questions coming from multiple interviewers.)

Small-group interviews may also be effective, particularly with a senior who is still mentally sharp and at ease with public speaking. A small group of younger interviewers might sit with the senior in a private setting—or the group interview might be done before a larger group, with the interviewers forming a panel that asks questions of a single older presenter. Alternatively, a panel of seniors might be invited to respond to a single interviewer or "questions from the audience."

A larger group setting is particularly conducive to submitting questions to the senior in advance and allowing him or her to prepare a presentation in response to those questions, whether in an educational or anecdotal fashion. This technique would benefit the entire church body—and it might be developed out of a prior process of more intimate interviews.

With whatever technique, supplying the senior member with the interview questions in advance will allow for more thoughtful, considered answers. For more extemporaneous responses, allow the questions to arise naturally out of the interview process—or keep some questions in reserve, to be broached only at the time of the interview or presentation. It is important to check with the presenter and follow the procedure that makes him or her most comfortable.

**TOPIC** The range of *topics* for discussion is very wide. Senior saints can speak to a wide variety of questions related to issues such as:

■ Birth—eliciting information about healthcare, black medical facilities and medical professionals, and practices such as midwifery and home birth.

■ Birthplace—descriptions of hometowns, life transitions, and historical events in context often create a vivid historical timeline.

■ Genealogy—producing a brief or detailed family history, including ancestors' birthplaces, education, and work, as well as values and traditions handed down through generations.

■ Education—describing the kind of education available, the nature of the school system, and the level of vocational training attained, including personal recollections of the buildings, classmates, teachers, courses, school rules, and social life.

■ Occupation—recounting the length of time on the job, skills needed, education required, range of work done, and barriers encountered or overcome.

■ Travel and transportation—recounting places they have traveled, modes of transportation, and memorable sites.

■ Family and childraising—answering how many children were in the family, the challenges in raising them, where their siblings are, and what they are doing now.

■ Food and meal preparation—sharing their favorite foods or family recipes, and describing types of kitchen utensils or tools that are now obsolete (e.g., sifters, grinders, hand-cranked churns).

■ Fashion and clothing—remembering old trends in clothing, accessories, hairstyles, and standards of modesty, perhaps including review of vintage photos.

■ Housing and living arrangements—describing former homes and living arrangements, particularly if they involved extended families, letting out rooms to boarders, etc.

■ Entertainment—sharing memories about popular entertainers from other eras, comparing and contrasting musical styles, as well as the range of social activities available "back in the day."

■ Church and religious activities—recalling oral church histories, including the evolution of a congregation and memories of prior pastors and old buildings or sites.

■ Philosophies of life—articulating how they have "come this far," and answering queries related to their outlooks on life, society, current issues, church, and other areas of interest.

**PRESENTATION AND PRESERVATION** The *presentation and preservation* portion of the storytelling project can be one of the most exciting and creative aspects of the entire venture. The mode chosen might be as simple as an audiotape collection of interviews or presentations. The audiotapes can also be transcribed and presented as a series of monthly or quarterly newsletters or compiled into a book form or binder. (If the church has desktop publishing capabilities, this project is even more feasible.)

Alternatively, or additionally, the interviews and presentations can be videotaped. These can be edited either in-house or through a video editing service. The end result would be a documentary-style keepsake for all members of the congregation.

Ideally, photos should be taken during the interviews or presentations. In that way, the faces as well as the words of the senior saints are preserved. These photos may be incorporated into the transcribed record or collected into a church album. If the church has the financial or in-house capabilities, a keepsake album could even be produced for each member of the congregation. Alternately, the members could order and pay separately.

Memories become more powerful with sensory impressions attached, so in addition to the visual complement of photographs, you might include with your senior memoirs some treasured recipes. This compilation could become a cookbook that chronicles the lives of the seniors in the church with recipes that evoke memories of former times—not to mention preserving the favorite tastes and aromas for generations to come.

Perhaps your congregation is more active than literary, in which case the young people might create, in conjunction with the youth minister or church drama coordinator, a stage play rendition of these stories. The younger people can reenact poignant scenes or monologues from the interviews or stories.

All of these ideas can work together to become an ongoing project or series of projects. The interviews or presentations can be worked onto the church calendar on a regular basis. Updated or companion videotapes, books, newsletters, and photos can be developed periodically and distributed throughout the congregation.

## "Tell Your Children and Grandchildren"

The power of story to shape individual lives and form community identity is undeniable. God himself commanded the people of Israel to retell their faith history as story to their children—"so that you may know that I am the LORD" (Exodus 10:2). It was a divine mandate that was both exhortation and cautionary.

As elderly members of the black community and their stories are welcomed in the church, with younger generations acting as conduits of those stories, three things will happen. First, the lives of the tellers and the hearers will become intertwined, and younger generations will begin to see the stories of the elderly as an essential part of their own story. They will become connected to their past, and the stories of the black experience in the United States of thirty, forty, sixty years ago will help shape the present-day identity of African American children, youth, adults, and faith communities.

Second, the experience of telling, hearing, and preserving these life stories will be a creative venture, bursting forth in new, shared stories of what it means to be a church of young, middle-aged, and older black Americans. In this way, story manifests its power not only to preserve but also to transform, grounded on the firm foundation of a faith-filled history.

And finally, younger people will come to see that they are themselves engaged in the process of creating what will be their own life stories. This experience of listening to and learning from the stories of others will empower them to both value and take charge of the situations and events that will comprise the story of their individual lives and the story of the corporate life of their church.

It is in the telling and receiving of these stories that the mutual benefits of caring for older blacks in the church is most apparent. The division between teller and hearer will be blurred as "their" stories and "our" lives merge to create a shared experience in which all participants are enriched and the life of the church is enhanced. Without ministry to and with our senior saints, churches cannot have a full identity. Without the full participation of the oldest members of your community, your church's story will be incomplete.

## Where Do You Stand?

1. What stories of an older generation have you heard?

2. What makes these stories so memorable?

3. What are some of your own stories?

4. Which of these stories would be edifying for a younger generation? Why?

## Models for Action

Create a storytelling model for your congregation by answering the following questions.

Which elderly members of your congregation would you interview?

■

■

- ■
- ■

In what setting would you conduct the interviews?

- ■
- ■
- ■
- ■

What interview techniques would you employ?

- ■
- ■
- ■
- ■

What topics would you cover?

- ■
- ■
- ■
- ■

How would you preserve and present the information?

- ■
- ■
- ■
- ■

# Facts and Figures

(Data compiled by the author from 1999, 2000, and 2001 statistics of the U.S. Census Bureau and 1999 reports from the Centers for Disease Control and Prevention)

FINANCES IN 1999:

■ Social Security accounted for nearly one-half of the total income for the black elderly (47.1%).

■ Retirement income from pensions ranked second (20%).

■ Earned income represented 17.7 %.

■ Social Security and Supplemental Security Income (SSI) accounted for one out of every two dollars of support for aged blacks.

■ One out of every nine (10.7%) received SSI.

■ One out of every eight (13.0%) had annual incomes below $5000.

■ One-half (49.9 percent) had annual income below $10,000

■ The median income was $9,766.

■ The unemployment rate for blacks 65 years and older was 5.0% (compared to 2.9% for whites 65 and older).

■ The Bureau of Census standard of annual income in 1999 classified individuals 65 or older with an income below $7,990 (or $10,075 for a married couple) as poor.

■ 1,551,000 elderly blacks could be classified as poor, marginally poor, or economically vulnerable.

## HEALTH AND LIFE EXPECTANCY

■ In October of 1999, the Centers for Disease Control and Prevention reported 39.9% of elderly blacks assessed their health status as poor or just fair.

■ Life expectancy at birth in 1998 for African American males was 67.6 years and for African American females 74.8 years.

■ If older blacks survive to age 65, their life expectancy beyond that age is 14.3 years for African American males and 17.4 years. for African American females (making possible a high percentage living to the age 79.3 and 82.4 years, respectively).

## POPULATION

■ In 2001, nearly three million (8.5 percent of all persons 65 or older) African Americans were 65 years of age or older.

■ From 1990–2000, the senior population increased in every state, ranging from a 1% increase in Rhode Island to a 72% increase in Nevada.

■ In the 1990s, the most rapid population growth took place in the oldest age group; the population 85 years and older increased by 38% (data compiled by the author from 1999, 2000, and 2001 statistics of the U.S. Census Bureau).

■ In 2000, there were 18.4 million people 65 to 74 years of age.

■ 39.5% of elderly blacks were male.

■ 60.5% of elderly blacks were female.

■ The elderly African American population is projected to grow by 89.6 % from 2001 to 2021.

■ The elderly black population is projected to grow by 220.4% from 2002 to 2041.

■ The survival rate of elderly black men is projected to improve to 42.4 % by year 2041.

■ Between the years 2001 and 2041, the African American elderly population is expected to increase by nearly three times that of the elderly white population.

PERCENTAGE OF BLACK ELDERLY IN POPULATIONS
OF SELECT STATES IN 2000
Alabama 13.0 %
Arkansas 14.0 %
Florida 17.6 %
Georgia 09.6 %
Illinois 12.1 %
Indiana 12.4 %
Kentucky 12.7 %
Louisiana 11.8%
Maryland 11.3 %
Michigan 12.3 %
Mississippi 12.1 %
North Carolina 12.0 %
Ohio 13.3 %
Oklahoma 12.8 %
South Carolina 12.1 %
Tennessee 9.9 %
Texas 12.4 %
Virginia 11.2 %

CITIES WITH HIGHEST PERCENTAGE OF
BLACK SENIOR ADULTS IN 2000
New York 11.7%
Los Angeles 9.7%
Chicago 10.3%
Houston 8.4%
Philadelphia 14.1%
Phoenix 8.1%
San Diego 10.5%
Dallas 8.6%
San Antonio 10.4%
Detroit 10.4%

# Opportunities Seized and Missed

I. More than twenty-three years ago the late Dr. Benjamin E. Mays made a simple request for a coat hanger in the bathroom of the Dean's Office of Morehouse School of Religion. During numerous meetings of the Executive Committee, he would remind me of how convenient a coat hanger would be for him. It was not an expensive investment, but the installation was never made. In the years since, I have learned the logic and urgency of Dr. Mays' request. My need to use public facilities in airports and hotel meeting areas has made it clear that it is inconvenient when there is no place to hang your suit jacket! The request had gone unheeded not as a budget issue, but because of a lack of sensitivity. Benjamin E. Mays left a significant gift to Morehouse School of Religion, including his home. I wonder if a coat hanger was ever installed in the bathroom of the Director's Office.

II. Mrs. Irene Dotson, the widow of Mr. George Dotson, who was surrogate father to many of the boys of our community, lived alone until her 87th year. The occasion of an intruder in her home required a residence change, which she strongly resisted. During a visit a year prior to her relocation to her daughter's home, she granted me entrance after identifying my voice. She explained that she was reluctant to open her door because she could not see the callers through the viewer with the front entrance light blown. Her rheumatoid arthritis prevented her from replacing the old bulb. I learned that the lamp had been blown for several months. She had light bulbs lying in the corner near the front door and any visitor could have remedied that situation, which had eroded her independence.

III. Mother Ida Compton, the widow of a minister who had lived in Atlanta with her husband for more than thirty years, returned to the small town of her earlier years and her home church. The move placed her in daily contact with her daughter's family, her grandchildren, and great grandchildren. With income from the sale of her Atlanta home, she financed add-on living space for herself to her daughter's home. In her mid-nineties, she was ambulatory and had keen mental ability. During a visit, I discerned pain and pathos in her otherwise pleasant countenance. She shared her disappointment in her living arrangements, which prompted an awareness in me of the need for housing options. The chair of the Board of Deacons and I began with consultation with the chair of the Deaconess Board to explore transitional housing options, should Mother Compton desire a change. We organized a housing committee and began to explore the possibility of a HUD-housing grant for two acres of church-owned land. Mother Compton's need for things was minimal, but her desire for the human touch of caring Christian fellowship was great. Peppermint candy was her only "material" request, and a financial gift was usually carefully pinned in the hem of her apron. Her greatest joy was found in the offering of a departing prayer by a visitor.

IV. Mother Leola Jordan's little home had a light fixture from which the socket was missing. The electric wire hung exposed with 110 volts of electrical power—low enough that the legally blind woman, who was less than five feet tall had to duck in order to avoid electric shock. When I inquired about the danger, Mother Jordan, who was never short on opinion and judgment, simply replied, "Reverend, it has been a danger long enough for some of your sorry deacons to see it, but they never noticed them wires. I guess they thought my old blind 'ass' would electrocute my old fool self. But I fooled them, didn't I? I ain't going before my God's good time…and I'll be ready when he comes for me!" Immediately upon my request, several men of the church made that simple repair. The cost for replacement wire and new fixtures was less than $3.50.

V. Miss Elizabeth Whitehead, a woman of meager means but royal vision, cultivated friends in church circles from coast to coast, and especially among ministers. She loved Spelman and Morehouse Colleges. She found it easy to ask persons of means for contributions and support for black higher education. Miss Whitehead lived to be a centenarian. She maintained her residence at great peril to her welfare, health, safety and security. Her "rugged individualism and pride" caused her to hold on at great risk. As a childless, single woman who survived all of her friends and acquaintances, her demise was fraught with confusion about her final wishes. Fortunately, the funeral director and her husband were trusted friends of Miss Whitehead. She had described what she expected to happen upon her death. However, the absence of documentation made plans unnecessarily awkward. In hindsight, it is clear that her younger friends may have missed a critical opportunity that would have allowed them to know about her final wishes.

VI. Several years ago members of the Board of Directors of the American Baptist Churches of the South observed and celebrated Holy Communion at the closing session of a meeting. The composition of that Board is representative of the region's membership. At one table sat a group of mature women representing the state of Florida and its congregations. For the closing communion service, disposable communion packets with the "bread and wine" in sealed in foil were used. The women from Florida encountered a barrier to their participation in the Lord's Supper. They struggled to open the communion packets, which required dexterity and strength in the fingers. I moved closer and helped with the packets, learning that "improvements" can create unintended barriers.

APPENDIX THREE

# Summary Recommendations

There is no monolithic typology that defines or describes African American communities or churches, so geography, denominational affiliation, polity, location, size, and economic climate must be factored into any planned ministries among the aging. The information presented in this book is offered with the hope of encouraging focused mission in African American churches in the interests of elderly blacks. A focus on aging in African American communities can potentially generate a movement that has implications for the advancement of African Americans in far reaching ways. The following conclusions and recommendations should serve to focus, challenge, and motivate pastors, lay leaders, and congregations in this critical ministry.

THREE BUILDING BLOCKS OF MINISTRY AMONG
AGING AFRICAN AMERICANS ARE:

■ sensitivity that leads to a heightened awareness of the presence, plight, and needs of the seniors in general and to everyday needs of those who have difficulty climbing stairs, hearing sermons, reading small print, and getting places

■ intentionality that insists on planned, executed, and evaluated interaction with the aging that leads to...

■ advocacy on the local, state, and national levels that may result in public policy changes, program initiation, and strategic location of services

MINISTRY AMONG THE ELDERLY IS CHARACTERIZED BY:
■ residual reciprocity in which all age groups benefit from one another's gifts and presence
■ information about the needs of the aged and the resources that are available on the community, state, and national levels
■ recognition that social structures that once supported generations within extended families are often stretched, or even nonexistent, in the context of modern life
■ training where necessary for those who seek to meet the needs of seniors and for seniors whose gifts need to be utilized within the faith community
■ people power with the recognition that this ministry is a ministry shared by all members of the congregation
■ hands-on leadership that recognizes the power of personal presence
■ respect for the wisdom, experience, and stories of those who have traveled many miles
■ partnerships for service among the elderly, adults, young adults, youth, and children

INITIAL CONSIDERATIONS FOR MINISTRY AMONG
AGING BLACKS INCLUDE:
■ the profile of aging blacks within your community
■ the predicament of and need for relief for day-to-day caregivers
■ the impact of "the sandwiched generation" and the capacity of particular family units to play the traditional role of care and support
■ focused areas of services for the elderly, such as adequate income, nutritional food, health care, housing, transportation, and legal counsel

# Select Resources for Ministry among the Elderly

## BOOKS

Malcolm Boyd, *Prayers for the Later Years* (Minneapolis: Augsburg Press, 2002).

Ursula Adler Falk and Gerhard Falk, *Grandparents: A New Look at the Supporting Generation* (Amherst, NY: Prometheus Books, 2001).

Marc Freedman, *Partners in Growth: Elder Mentors and At-Risk Youth* (New York, Philadelphia, Oakland: Public/Private Ventures, 1988).

Meredith Minkler and Kathleen M. Roe, *Grandmothers as Caregivers: Raising Children of the Crack Cocaine Epidemic* (Newbury Park, CA: Sage Publications, 1993).

James C. Perkins, *Building Up Zion's Walls: Ministry for Empowering the African American Family* (Valley Forge, PA: Judson Press, 1999).

Leslie J. Pollard, *Complaint to the Lord: Historical Perspectives on the African American Elderly* (Selinsgrove, PA: Susquehanna University Press, 1996).

Robert E. Seymour, *Aging without Apology: Living the Senior Years with Integrity and Faith* (Valley Forge, PA: Judson Press, 1995).

Henry Simmons, *Soulful Aging: Ministry Through the Stages of Adulthood* (Macon, GA: Smith and Helwys, 2001).

Anne Streaty Wimberly, ed., *Honoring African American Elders: A Ministry in the Soul Community* (New York: Jossey-Bass, 1997).

Edward P. Wimberly, *Claiming God: Reclaiming Dignity—African American Pastoral Care* (Nashville: Abingdon, 1991).

ORGANIZATIONS
*American Health Assistance Foundation*: Gives grants to Alzheimer's patients and caregivers to help with expenses. Contact: American Health Assistance Foundation, 22512 Gateway Center Dr., Clarksburg MD 20871, (301) 948-3244, http://www.ahaf.org.

*Black Elderly Legal Assistance Support Project*: Stimulates the involvement of local chapters of the National Bar Association to establish and expand African American and other minority community care coalitions at four sites around the nation. Outcomes are targeted to the legal assistance needs of African American and other minority elderly. Contact: Black Elderly Legal Assistance Support Project, c/o National Bar Association, 1225 11th Street, N.W., Washington, DC 20001, (202) 842-3900.

*Community Connections Clearinghouse*: The information center for the Office of Community Planning and Development (CPD) at the U.S. Department of Housing and Urban Development. The Center serves CPD, its clients and customers, and all those with a common interest in safe, decent, affordable housing, and those interested in creating community and economic development opportunities at the local level. Contact: Community Connections Clearinghouse, P.O. Box 7189, Gaithersburg MD 20898, (800) 998-9999, http://www.comcon.org.

*Department of Veterans Affairs*: Offers long-term healthcare for senior veterans to ensure they have the best possible home healthcare and end of life care. They have a facility locator on their website so searchers can find the locations nearest to them. Contact: http://www.va.gov.

*Medicare Assistance for Nursing Home Costs*: The official U.S. government website for people with Medicare, providing people with helpful information about healthcare programs and benefits. Contact: http://www.medicare.gov/nursing/payment.asp.

*The National Caucus and Center on Black Aged Inc.*: Throughout its thirty-four year history, the Washington, D.C. based National Caucus and Center on Black Aged, Inc. has worked to eliminate obstacles to fairness and equal access for one of the most underserved and vulnerable groups in our society—low-income black and minority senior citizens. The NCBA has one mission: to improve the quality of life for elderly African Americans and other minorities. Its programs have focused on three of the most critical needs: housing, employment and health promotion/disease prevention. NCBA has a well-earned reputation as the national leader in assuring that minority elders are represented at the national, state and local policy levels. Contact: (202) 637-8400, http://www.ncba-aged.org/about/history/index.html info@ncba-aged.org

*National Council on the Aging*: Their website includes information on the National Interfaith Coalition on Aging (NICA). NICA's pages on the website offer the original definition of "spiritual well-being," as well as a history of this important term and other useful resources. Contact: http://www.ncoa.org.

*Pension Benefit Guarantee Corporation*: Established by the federal government to protect pensions from private companies. Many people who are entitled to a pension from former employers don't know it. You can search by name, company, and location at the PBGC website to see if you, a family member, or a friend has an unclaimed pension. Contact: Pension Benefit Guarantee Corporation, 1200 K Street, NW, Washington, DC 20005-4026, (202) 326-4000, http://www.pbgc.gov/search/srchpension.htm.

*The Rural Housing Service*: Provides a number of homeowner opportunities to rural Americans, as well as programs for home renovation and repair. RHS also makes financing available to elderly, disabled, or low-income rural residents of multi-unit housing buildings to ensure they are able to make rent payments. Their website lists office locations around the country. Contact: http://www.rurdev.usda.gov/rhs/common/indiv_intro.htm.

*The Thanks Be To Grandmother Winifred Foundation*: Gives grants to women over 54 years of age to develop and implement programs that empower and enrich the lives of women. Contact: P.O. Box 1449, Wainscott, NY 11975, (516) 728-0323, http://www.csuohio.edu/uored/FUNDING/GrandmotherWinifred .html.

*Weatherization Assistance Programs Branch, EE44*: If you meet certain income guidelines, you may be allotted money to insulate your home or apartment, put in storm windows, and even pay for weather stripping, all of which can reduce your fuel bill. Each year states give money to nonprofit organizations that provide these kinds of services. Families with senior citizens (or young children) living in their homes take priority when it comes to these grants, which average about $2,000. Contact: Weatherization Assistance Programs Branch, EE44, c/o U.S. Department of Energy, 1000 Independence Avenue, SW, Washington, DC 20585, (202) 586-4074 or (800) DIAL-DOE.